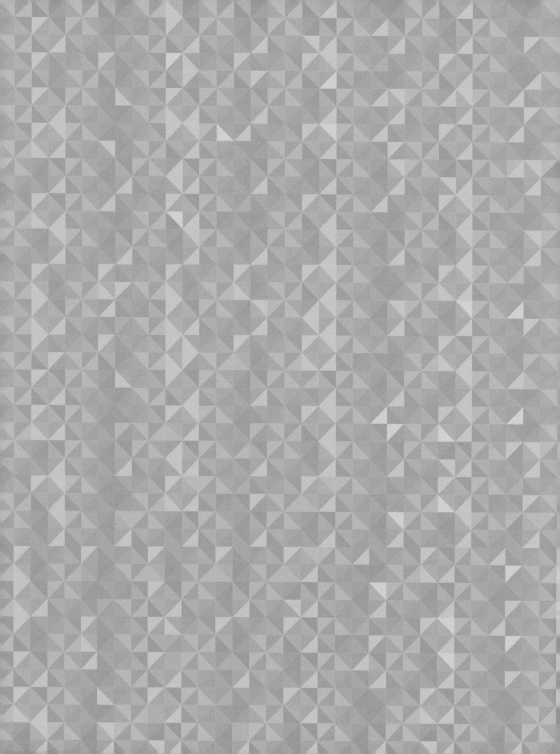

HOME SWEET RENTED HOME

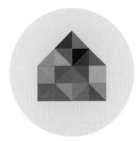

HOME SWEET RENTED HOME

TRANSFORM YOUR HOME
WITHOUT LOSING YOUR DEPOSIT

MEDINA GRILLO

MITCHELL BEAZLEY

This book is dedicated to all the renters whose landlords said they couldn't…

An Hachette UK Company
www.hachette.co.uk

First published in Great Britain in 2019 by Mitchell Beazley, an imprint of Octopus Publishing Group Ltd
Carmelite House, 50 Victoria Embankment
London EC4Y 0DZ
www.octopusbooks.co.uk

Text copyright © Medina Grillo 2019
Specially commissioned photography, on pages 67, 99, 105, 109, 113, 145, 153, 165 and 181, copyright © Kasia Fiszer 2019
Design, layout and illustration copyright © Octopus Publishing Group Ltd 2019

Distributed in the US by Hachette Book Group
1290 Avenue of the Americas, 4th and 5th Floors
New York, NY 10104

Distributed in Canada by Canadian Manda Group
664 Annette St., Toronto, Ontario, Canada M6S 2C8

ISBN 978-1-78472-600-3

A CIP catalogue record for this book is available from the British Library.

Printed and bound in China
10 9 8 7 6 5 4 3 2 1

Additional photography:
Alamy Stock Photo Melany Wood-Pearce 139.
Gap Interior Images Bureaux/Warren Heath 161; Dan Duchars 131; Rachel Whiting 29.
Getty Images Charlie Dean 77; Chemistry 71; Oscar Wong 121; Richard Fraser 125; Richard Powers/Arcaid 43; Silke Zander 143.
Giulia Hetherington 179.
Haarala Hamilton 20.
Homewings x Habitat, photography by Ash James 65.
iStock ALEAIMAGE 187; eriyalim 39; KatarzynaBialasiewicz 15, 45, 59, 127.
living4media Marij Hessel 63.
Kasia Fiszer 117
Lou Rowland "Face print" in photograph on page 105
Loupe Images Debi Treloar 41, 84, 159; Emma Mitchell & James Gardiner 103, 175; Jan Baldwin 83; Rachel Whiting 23; Simon Brown 50, 171.
Medina Grillo 7, 13, 31, 33, 49, 53, 73, 81, 95, 149, 157
Unsplash Avery Klein 137; Christopher Jolly 122; Jason Briscoe 19; John Mark Arnold 141.
www.habitat.co.uk 2, 27, 89, 91.

Special thanks to Habitat.co.uk and Ikea.com for their contribution to this book.

Velcro is a registered trademark.

Commissioned by: Ella Parsons
Creative Director: Jonathan Christie
Designer: Matt Cox at Newman+Eastwood
Illustrator: Ella Mclean
Copy Editor: Katy Denny
Production Manager: Nic Jones

For specially commissioned photography:
Photographer: Kasia Fiszer
Prop Stylist: Lauren Law

NOTES ON SAFETY

Keep your tools clean and well maintained. Make sure you thoroughly inspect the equipment before use, and store them appropriately (away from the reach of children).

Make sure you are comfortable with the equipment. If in any doubt – consult or even hire a professional.

Always secure movable objects or materials with clamps or a vice, freeing both hands to operate the tool.

Wear protective glasses. If using a sander, make sure to wear a protective face mask/ventilator to prevent any dust or debris affecting your lungs.

Every effort has been made to ensure that all the information in this book is accurate. However, due to differing conditions, tools, and individual skills, the publisher cannot be responsible for any injuries, losses, and other damages that may result from the use of the information in this book.

CONTENTS

INTRODUCTION

Ever since I can remember, I have always wanted to write a book. Of course, I just didn't know it would be this type of book.

As a child, I would spend hours bringing fictional characters to life on my typewriter – a gift I had persuaded my mum was a necessity for all great authors. Yes, *great* authors. I was going to be the next JK Rowling for sure. One of my earliest memories is of myself, aged seven, sharing passages from stories I had written with my dad. I would get so excited reading the words out loud to him that I often wouldn't realize he had dozed off. When I did, it would be a quick nudge and a whiny wail: 'Dad! Are you listening? This is the best part!'

He'd wake up with a start. 'Yes, yes,' he'd insist with a wide smile, 'I'm listening, sorry, go on. Your voice is just so relaxing.'

Not much has changed. I'm still often told that I should lend my voice to one of those sleep-inducing audio books, and dad still likes to doze off in various spots around the house. But I *have* finally written a book. And, even better, it is about something I have become so passionate about: the art of decorating, when your home isn't technically 'yours'.

This book is a dedication to all sorts of renters out there – whether that be short-term, long-term or most-likely-renting-for-life-term (like me). It's also a dedication to the old me.

Old me was a little ashamed to tell anyone that she was renting because, surely, at age 30, married with a kid, she should own a house by now. Old me was obsessed with saving for a deposit, always putting off decorating, never appreciating the joys of the here and now. Old me was constantly looking to the future and that dream of someday getting onto the property ladder. Old me never really loved the homes she rented, which was strange because the older she got, the more time she spent indoors. Old me *needed* this book.

Thankfully, old me has since progressed to current me. And current me has a new outlook on life as a renter. So you don't own your own home? That's OK. Or maybe your landlord isn't the easiest or the most open-minded? That's OK too. You can still create a home you love, a home that makes you feel happy and content the moment you walk through that door. Above all, a home that tells a story and celebrates YOU: your style, your personality, your family.

I kid you not. It is possible.

Hence this book.

I hope you'll enjoy reading it as much as I have enjoyed writing it.

Medina

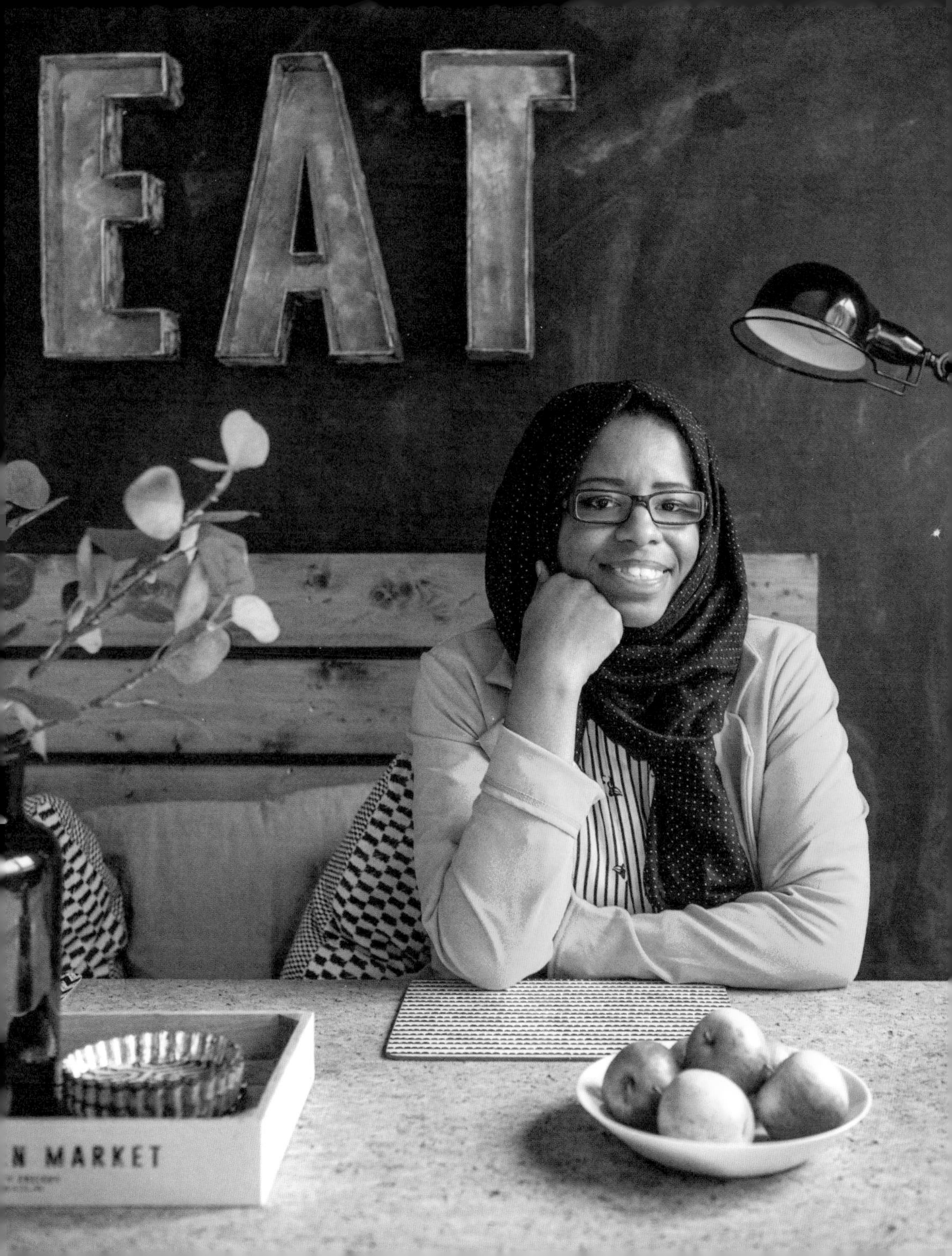
EAT
N MARKET

MAKE YOUR HOUSE A HOME

When I first started renting (I'm taking you back to the early 2000s here), Pinterest wasn't a thing, and certainly the idea to browse a blog for inspiration never occurred to me.

This meant that I barely decorated any of the properties I lived in because I lacked the inspiration needed for the execution. My walls were often left untouched, devoid of any colour or indication that someone with a personality lived there.

It was always, 'Well I won't do that – just in case it ruins the wall.' Or 'That looks great but I just don't think it will work for me – maybe when I have my own home?' Looking back, I wish I had been a little more experimental with my choices. I wish I hadn't wasted so much time dreaming about an 'if', when 'now' had been just as worthy of my attention.

There had been a designer inside me, itching to come out, but I had kept her restrained, shackled by my own insecurities.

However, things have changed…

1. I've stopped preoccupying myself with the idea that my happiness is dependent on whatever might lie ahead in the future (in this case, buying a house). Contentment within my home is something I can find now – but only if I allow myself to actually appreciate the act of real living.

2. I've set that inner designer free.

3. Pinterest and Instagram are providing a good chunk of my daily inspiration.

And now I'm here to share what I've learned with you.

> *Contentment within your home is something you can find now, not in a far-off, home-owning future.*

In my experience, there are three types of landlords:

1. Those who are totally against you making any type of superficial alteration to the house or apartment (such as putting nails in the walls or painting). This type of landlord is typical of student accommodation, privately rented properties or military housing. The rules on decorating are very rigid and periodic house inspections are carried out to ensure these rules are being followed.

2. Those who don't mind you decorating as long as you don't do anything too alarming and everything is returned back to its original condition upon leaving. This is really important if you wish to get your security deposit back with a good reference for your next tenancy.

3. Those who are completely fine with you decorating. These landlords may even see your painting as a way to upgrade the look of the rented property. In this case, you usually do not have to paint everything back when you leave, but, again, it's all about communication and obtaining written consent.

So, when decorating your rented home, *always* bear your landlord in mind. Throughout this book you will find projects that are 'full-on renter friendly', others that will need to be returned to their original state, and some that will require permission from the landlord. Start with the smaller tips and inspiration, and build up to the larger projects as your confidence grows.

EXPLORE AND EXPERIMENT

I should mention that although I write about interiors, decorate my rented home (a touch obsessively) and upcycle furniture, I am not a professional interior designer or decorator.

So, while using these pages as inspiration, experiment with your own style. Be bold with colour, explore different patterns and, most importantly, let your personality shine. It's your home. Make it yours.

WALLS

I can still remember the very first apartment my husband and I went to view. More specifically, I remember the walls.

The peeling, embossed wallpaper in the kitchen, the stained floorboards in the bedroom and the seemingly endless stretches of grubby magnolia paintwork on the walls. (There was also a small damp patch on the living room ceiling, but that was a minor detail in comparison.)

Let's talk about the magnolia, though. It was on Every. Single. Wall. In Every. Single. Room. And it had a nauseatingly yellowish shade to it that made me feel slightly ill.

'Lots of magnolia!' I remember saying to the agent (realtor) with a little frown. As if he didn't know.

He just shrugged nonchalantly. He did know, and me bluntly stating the obvious had clearly annoyed him.

'Are we allowed to paint the walls?' This was another question I couldn't help asking. You have to understand, I was new to house-hunting.

'Yes,' he replied, looking me straight in the eyes. 'Magnolia'.

Fast-forward to present day, and you could say I've become a little savvier and a heck of a lot more resourceful when it comes to injecting my personality on rented walls (in a non-intrusive way). Of course, this newfound wisdom and possibly skill (which I can only imagine I acquired from my serial-renter lifestyle) also includes the art of compromise – such as learning how to live with magnolia walls and not hating the colour as much.

All right, that's only half true – I'll always hate the colour.

The following chapter will cover all things wall décor. I'm going to be showing you a variety of creative things you can do to make your magnolia or bland white walls less of a bore. Most of these ideas are full-on renter friendly, but a few may require minimal effort to return the walls to the original state at the end of your tenancy.

WHY YOU NEED A GALLERY WALL IN YOUR LIFE

You don't necessarily need to whip out a paintbrush to add character to a space. One of the easiest ways to make a house or apartment feel truly like your own is to hang things up on the wall. In other words, create an awesome gallery wall.

A gallery wall is an amazing way to infuse colour and pattern into an otherwise empty room. It also allows you to group together and very cleverly display collections in a way that shows who you are and what you love.

Will gallery walls ever go out of fashion?
Absolutely not!

Although, on second thoughts, what do I really know about interior trends? Not much as it happens. But I am confident that gallery walls are here to stay.

So why?

They are budget-friendly – especially if you go down the vintage or upcycled route. Just one tip: frames can sometimes be costly, so buying in bulk from a charity shop or thrift store will save you money. You can then spray-paint them all the same colour.

Gallery walls can be created anywhere and everywhere. You could have one above your bed, as a focal point in your living room, next to your kitchen table, up the side of the stairs, around your television… Maybe I should have listed where they can't go!

HOW TO ACHIEVE A RENTER-FRIENDLY GALLERY WALL

Your next question might well be: but how exactly is nailing frames and/or other objects to the wall renter-friendly?

Let me explain, in just two words:

Adhesive Strips.

Actually, I'm going to make that three words:

Revolutionary Adhesive Strips.

These are a specialized kind of tape with an adhesive backing that come in a variety of sizes and forms. They are perfect for hanging items with a flat back, such as pictures and frames. When applied properly, these strips can later be removed from the wall without leaving any damage or residue behind.

I should also add here that as well as adhesive strips, there are products such as heavy-duty Velcro that can be used to hang items or pictures. These work particularly well for items you plan to remove from the wall often.

Just a few things to remember when using adhesive strips:

● Always check that the product you're using is suitable for the weight of what you want to hang (there are a few brands out there, and each one is different).

● Make sure the adhesive product you choose is right for the surface on which you're intending to hang something. Most require a smooth, clean wall. As a result, this product might not work on bumpy, uneven walls or wallpaper.

● If your wall has been freshly painted, wait a few weeks before applying these strips – check the manufacturer's guidelines for exactly how long to wait.

● When trying to remove stubborn strips from the wall, apply a little heat with a hairdryer for 20–30 seconds and then cut through the adhesive with a piece of dental floss.

> *Let me explain, in just two words:*
> *Adhesive Strips*

Now that we have established there is, indeed, a magic tool that makes hanging pictures a heck of a lot easier, here are a few gallery-hanging basics that you should probably know.

DO

1. Try creating a mood board before you start. Are you going to mix it up, or go for a more streamlined effect? Will the gallery wall be symmetrical or asymmetrical?

2. Start with the largest frame and build a variety of different frames around that.

3. Keep to a theme – whether colour, texture or subject. This will help ensure your gallery wall looks cohesive.

4. Lay your gallery out on the floor to finalize the arrangement before you commit to mounting it on the wall. Takea quick photo with your phone so that you don't forget the layout.

DON'T

1. Forget to use a spirit level to ensure all your pictures are hung straight. There's nothing worse than a gallery wall with crooked frames (unless, of course, that is the look you are going for).

2. Get too caught up in the method or excessively overthink it. If it looks right to you, it probably is. Allow your creativity to flow. (I hope I haven't just contradicted myself here.)

MORE GALLERY WALL IDEAS

WASHI TAPE FRAMES

Washi tape (made from Japanese paper) is quite similar to masking tape and is super-durable and flexible. It is available in a variety of widths, textures, patterns and colours. It tears easily and can be safely applied to an array of surfaces without leaving any residue behind. Use washi tape to:

1. Simply hang your pictures.
2. Create stylish and colourful frames for your artwork or photos.
3. Give your walls a pop of colour and design an interesting feature wall.

BASKETS OR OTHER DECORATIVE ITEMS

From textiles to jewellery, and sometimes even straw hats and baskets, gallery walls are just a tad more interesting and dynamic when you ditch the traditional 2-D flat look and add a few multi-dimensional objects into the mix such as straw hats or vintage tins.

CLIPBOARDS

You can attach clipboards to the wall with adhesive strips or hooks. This is a clever way to change or rotate art or photos.

I want to say the sky is the limit because it (almost) is…

WHAT TO PUT INSIDE PICTURE FRAMES

Anything goes – and by 'anything', I mean anything! Look for features or colours that already exist in a room and play off that.

Here are just a few ideas:

- Decorative tea (dish) towels
- Personal photos
- Vintage newspaper clippings
- Printed art or typography
- Fabric scraps
- Wallpaper samples
- Abstract art

HANGING PICTURES WITH WIRE AND PEGS

Attach wire or string to the wall with adhesive hooks and use pegs to display your photos or prints.

HANGING PICTURES WITH CLOTHES HANGERS

This might sound a little long-winded, but hanging pictures using the type of clothes hangers that have integral clips is actually really aesthetically pleasing. You can use vintage wooden hangers suspended from adhesive hooks.

DISPLAYING PICTURES USING PICTURE LEDGES

This is a little more intrusive as you will need to drill a few screw holes to make this possible (remember, you will need to fill them in at the end of your tenancy). You'll be able to display art (or even books) and change the arrangement around without having to put up new hooks or adhesive strips.

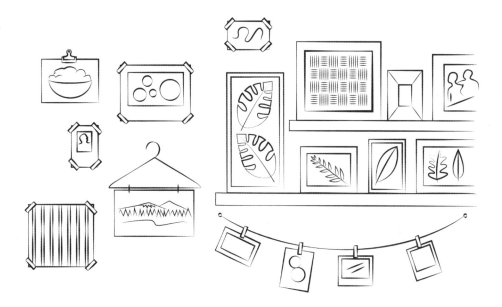

GALLERY WALL USING RUGS AND/OR MACRAMÉ

Macramé, the knot-tying craft enjoyed by so many in the Seventies, has made a bit of a comeback – in particular, macramé and woven wall hangings. And why not?

Even though they are mostly neutral in colour, they still add texture and dimension to a wall, and are renter-friendly as they can be hung from self-adhesive hooks. There are many tutorials online for how to make your own, or you can buy handmade examples from independent stores.

Similarly, maybe you have a colourful Persian rug that you picked up on your travels and want to display? You don't have space on the floor for another rug, but your walls are empty and crying out to be dressed with something, anything!

The best way to hang a rug is by using Velcro tape, which consists of two separate strips: the hook tape and the loop tape. The loop tape needs to be sewn (or glued) to the top of the rug on the reverse. The hook tape can then be applied directly to the wall. But please note, this method will only work with lightweight rugs; heavier rugs will need to be hung using a curtain pole.

MIRROR GALLERY WALL

Well, OK, maybe not an entire wall of mirrors (mirrors can be quite heavy and often require wall screws to secure them in place), just one or two will do. You won't regret it, I promise! Not only do mirrors look great, but they also help to reflect light and make small spaces feel larger.

Adhesive strips can be used to temporarily hang lightweight mirrors to the wall. You can also buy mirrors that come with a self-adhesive backing and stick them to your walls – or doors.

AND TO END ON A SLIGHTLY DIFFERENT NOTE

You don't always have to hang something on the wall to create a gallery.

- Leaning really large-scale framed art, painted canvases, mirrors or industrial letters against the walls or propping them up against the back of sturdy furniture such as a sofa can be a great look.

- An old shutter, window, door, or even a thick sheet of stained plywood can be propped against a wall to display a collage of personal photos, cards and prints. Attach a little hook to the wall above and a strong cord to the back of your board, then loop the card around the hook to anchor the board in place so it doesn't fall over.

THE DREADED PAINT CLAUSE IN THE CONTRACT

You've seen a house you absolutely love. It's a great size, in the perfect location and, most importantly, it's clean and well maintained. 'I'll take it,' you say, without even having to think twice.

A few days later, you find yourself sitting in the letting agent's (realtor's) office. You're a little nervous, but the agent is nice, takes time to reassure you, and hands you the paperwork. You start off by casually flicking through its pages, but then suddenly recall reading somewhere about how important it is to know exactly what you are signing up to before actually signing your name on the line. And so you realize you had better do just that.

You read a lot of jargon that mostly goes over your head, but there is one clause that stands out. It reads something like: 'tenants are not allowed to decorate or paint, or change the internal structure of the property in any way.' Your heart sinks because you know exactly what that means. You sign the paper anyway and the house is yours. The end. Or maybe not…

Most contracts will have a similar sentence or paragraph, which is usually there to manage a tenant's expectations as well as to cover the landlord's back, should there ever be a need for them to claim funds from the security deposit.

The good news? It's not always set in stone.

And, honestly, it really doesn't hurt to ask.

There are occasions when a landlord may give permission for you to decorate (mostly in longer term leases) with set terms and conditions (for example, repainting at the end of the tenancy). It really just depends on your relationship with your landlord. I would strongly suggest sitting down with him or her for a general chat first, before even thinking about asking to paint.

" *Your heart sinks because you know exactly what that means. You sign the paper anyway and the house is yours. The end. Or maybe not...* **"**

The idea is to be open and honest with your landlord about your potential plans and ideas. Discuss things such as choice of colours, types of paint, whether you will be doing the painting yourself or getting an expert in to help. Try to sell the idea that these changes will be a good thing and will only enhance the property further.

There are really only three ways this conversation can go.

1. He or she say yes, but on condition that they are consulted throughout the whole painting process. Maybe they'll want you to use only neutral colours that they have already approved. This is slightly limiting but it does mean that there is a good chance you won't have to make any drastic changes when you decide to leave.

2. He or she say yes, but they want you to return everything to its original state once you leave. You basically have free rein here. Word of warning, though – don't get too carried away. It's all fun and games until you find yourself, when you do move out, rushing to slap on a second layer of primer to a wall that had previously been painted black.

3. They'll say sorry but no, not a chance! Not the answer any of us want to hear but, remember, there are other options. And I'll be discussing them throughout the book.

Finally, your willingness to compromise is key.

NOTE

Did I mention that getting the landlord's permission down in writing is super-important? Vital, in fact, because should anything untoward happen, I'm afraid that simply saying 'he/she said I could' won't stand up in court.

TO PAINT OR NOT TO PAINT?

For some people, being told that they are allowed to paint, but that they have to return the walls to their original state upon leaving, is a double-edged sword. And it begs the question: is it really worth the time and effort?

In trying to justify the desire to paint, here are some of the questions I ask myself. Maybe you'll find these helpful, too.

How much will it cost? (Remember to factor in the cost of painting it back to the original colour.)

How bad is the current paint colour?

Is the current wall colour significantly hampering my ability to feel at peace and at home in this house?

Will painting this wall or room improve my overall experience here?

Will it make me feel happy?

How long do I see myself living here?

It is very rare for me to get to the bottom of this list of questions and still feel undecided about whether I am going to paint or not. Firstly, because I tell myself that painting a wall, in the grand scheme of things, really isn't that big a deal. Secondly, because it is without a doubt, the easiest way to jazz up your home.

You just need to follow a few tips so you don't end up annoying your landlord and losing your security deposit altogether.

PAINTING TIPS

TRY 'OTHER' NEUTRAL COLOURS

I'm sure you've probably realized by now that magnolia isn't a favourite colour of mine (is it anyone's, really?). However, it can be a popular colour with landlords, maybe because it's a warm neutral that is light enough to make spaces seem large and warm enough to give a cosy feel. But why not choose another shade from the neutral palette, such as white? This will contrast well with your furniture and help give small spaces a more spacious feel. Also, as it's a neutral colour, it's unlikely that you will have to paint the wall back to whatever colour it was before, although do check before you paint.

LESS IS MORE

Ask yourself – do you really need to paint an entire room a bold colour? Bolder colour choices will require more priming and at least two layers of top coat, should you ever need to repaint. Sometimes painting just one wall (creating a feature wall) or even a ceiling with a bold colour or pattern, and leaving the rest of the walls neutral, can make an equally dramatic difference.

BE SMART AND PROTECT

This is particularly important if you are renting a furnished home. You really don't want to risk splattering (or spilling) paint on the more permanent fixtures.

Use old sheets, covers and cloths to protect furniture and flooring. I remember once leaving a huge gloss paint stain on the carpet in a previous rental property. I couldn't remove it (and I tried literally everything!) so the landlord took a fee from my deposit. I wasn't pleased, but it was only fair.

CHOOSE PAINTS WITH THE RIGHT FINISH

Matt or eggshell paints are great for concealing surface flaws on walls that are patchy or cracking. The glossier paint reflects more light and highlights any imperfections. However, matt walls are a little harder to maintain and keep clean. Every mark or fingerprint WILL show up – eventually, you might find yourself in the position of having to repaint the whole wall again (or at the very least, having to do regular touchups). For this reason, they work much better in low-traffic areas such as the bedroom.

Satin or semi-gloss paints are far more practical for high-traffic areas such as the living room and hallways. Marks can easily be wiped off. The only downside is that this type of paint can sometimes show brush/roller strokes and might look a little shiny.

Two pairs of hands really are better than one. Bribe some friends with the promise of free pizza if they help you paint.

EXPERIMENT

If you're wanting to create an exciting look with as little effort as possible, experiment by trying out different paint designs for feature walls. You could try stencilled walls, half-painted walls, stripes, ombre effects, and so on.

GET A FRIEND TO HELP

It's probably obvious, but two pairs of hands really are better than one. Bribe some friends with the promise of free pizza if they help – unless you're a perfectionist and like things done a certain way, as it's hard to control quality when more hands are involved. You don't want to lose friends over what was intended as a semi-social helping hand.

WHAT IS REMOVABLE WALLPAPER?

Only the best thing since sliced bread.

Removable wallpaper – which goes by lots of other names, including peel-and-stick wallpaper, renters' paper and temporary wallpaper – is a paper with an adhesive backing that can be attached to walls without the need for traditional wallpaper paste or water activation to secure it in place.

It is, essentially, a new and improved (some might say fancier) version of sticky-back vinyl (contact paper) and is marketed specifically for walls. However, there are occasions when it can also be used on non-wall surfaces such as furniture, which I'll touch on later.

And if you've ever been tasked with the mind-numbingly tedious chore of removing traditional wallpaper (steamer and scraper at the ready!), I can guarantee that you'll very much appreciate these next few sentences.

There's a spoiler in the name really.

Removable wallpaper can be peeled off walls with very little effort and does not cause any damage. In other words, you are free to add a touch of refinement and a new dimension to your home without the consequence of permanence – a complete ten out of ten on that imaginary renter-friendly scale. And with lots of new developments in terms of design, there are now tons of styles, patterns and finishes of removable wallpaper to choose from.

Finally, in case you're concerned about cost, you'll be pleased to know that removable wallpaper works out to be the same, if not slightly cheaper, than the traditional kind (depending on the brand and where in the world you live). This is because most removable wallpaper is custom-made and cut to your precise measurements. Not having to guesstimate when buying rolls means that you are paying for the exact amount that you actually need.

Less waste, too, which is always a good thing.

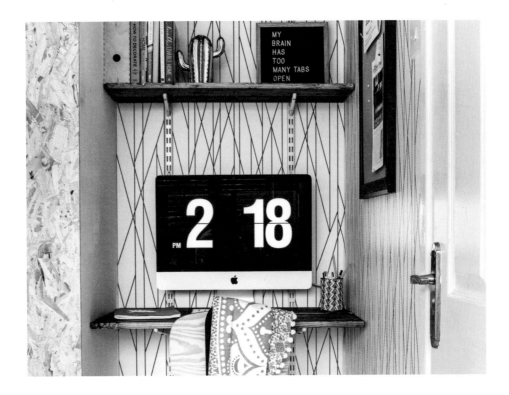

PROS

- Often works out cheaper than traditional high-quality wallpaper
- Much cleaner application
- Application process does not require as much space
- Can easily be removed and adjusted
- No damage caused to the wall
- Less waste
- Can be reused – if you remember to keep the backing

CONS

- Can't be applied to all walls (for example, textured or bumpy walls)
- The print and paper quality can sometimes feel a little different from traditional wallpaper

PROJECT #1

HOW TO APPLY REMOVABLE WALLPAPER

Are you sold on this magical stuff yet? Hoping that's a big fat yes! Right, let's get on to the fun part – how to apply it. Please note that these are general guidelines. Most of the time, removable wallpaper comes with its own set of instructions for application, so make sure those take precedence.

SUPPLIES

- Spirit level
- Pencil
- Removable wallpaper (no-brainer)
- Ruler/tape measure
- Stepladder (take care and ask someone to hold it steady)
- Old bank or store card
- Craft knife or scalpel
- Scissors
- Extra pair of hands (highly recommended)

Before you start:

- Order a few samples of the removable paper before you buy. Apply the samples to the wall and see how they look throughout the day, to assess the quality and general feel of the paper – and, most importantly, to decide whether the design or pattern will look good on your wall.
- Make sure you take the measurements of your wall correctly. Measure more than once. To allow for error, always add a few centimetres to these measurements. There is nothing worse than starting this process and half-way through, realizing you haven't ordered enough.
- Ensure your wall is smooth, without any holes, cracks or bumps. Repair, fill and sand down as need be.
- If you have recently painted your walls, it's usually necessary to wait at least four weeks before applying removable wallpaper. And if there is already wallpaper on the wall, that will need to be removed first.
- If you are applying this wallpaper in the kitchen or bathroom, where there is more risk of humidity and water exposure, you may want to buy a removable paper with a glossy finish that can be wiped over with a damp cloth. However, it's always best to check the exact specifications and durability with the manufacturer. Or, once the wallpaper has been applied to the wall, you could seal it with a coat of clear varnish (polyurethane).

1

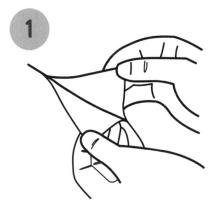

2

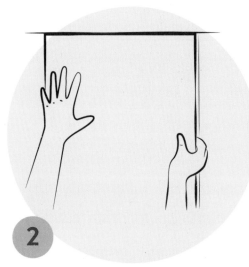

Use your spirit level and a pencil to draw a vertical line as a reference. Do not automatically assume that your walls, door frames or skirting boards (baseboards) are straight – especially in older houses.

Beginning at a top corner, remove the wallpaper from the backing – but only about 5cm (2in) at a time. This paper is extremely sticky, so if you remove too much at once, the paper will somehow find a way to stick to itself (it is super-annoying when that happens).

Line the paper up against your vertical line and fix the top corner. Smooth the paper firmly into the corner with either your hand or bank card. The 'exposed' part should stick to the wall.

3

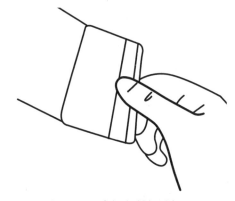

Once the top corner is secure, reach behind the paper and pull away more of the backing, making sure to smooth with your card as you go. Pull the backing down at a 45-degree angle until the whole of the top is stuck to the wall. Then continue downward, smoothing from the centre outward to push air bubbles out to the edges. The paper can be lifted up and pressed down again, should you encounter an air bubble that doesn't seem to want to shift. For really stubborn air bubbles, make a small slit in the

paper at the centre of the bubble with your craft knife or scalpel, then smooth it down. This process is quite fiddly, especially if you are using large pieces of wallpaper, so having someone to assist you can make all the difference.

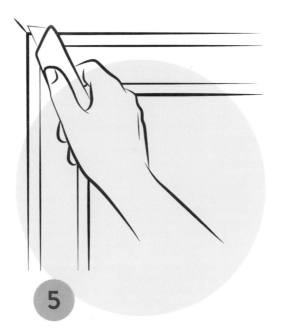

4

There should be no need to overlap the wallpaper because it is usually designed to match up perfectly. Just line up your second piece with the top half of the first and repeat the sticking process. Continue with all the pieces until your wall is completely covered.

5

If you need to go around a window frame, light switch or door frame, make a few small cuts at each corner with your knife or scalpel, and smooth the wallpaper into the crease.

6

Trim the excess edges of the paper. To do this, place a ruler against the edge of the wall, on top of the paper, and slowly run your knife along that line, then peel away the excess paper.

AND TO REMOVE...

Simply peel off a corner and pull away.

WHERE TO HANG REMOVABLE WALLPAPER

Removable wallpaper is often applied to just one wall to create a feature wall. However, there are many other creative ways it can be used on your walls.

Of course, a whole room can be wallpapered. This makes for quite a dramatic, maximalist look, especially if you are using a bold pattern or print. But proceed with caution, as you can run the risk of it looking too busy. Perhaps counterintuitively, this method works very effectively in smaller spaces such as a laundry room, toilet or porch (foyer).

However, you don't have to commit to wallpapering an entire room (or an entire wall). Here are some other options:

1. Wallpaper only the top half of a wall. This looks particularly good above any existing wall panelling.

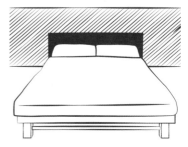

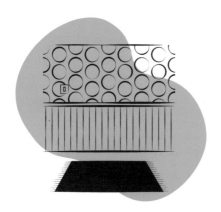

2. Apply paper to just the bottom part of a wall. In a bedroom, this could act as a faux headboard, depending on the design of paper you choose.

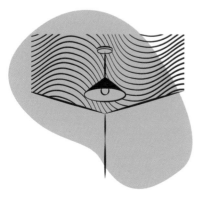

5. Wallpaper always looks great applied to the inside of an alcove.

3. You could try applying wallpaper to the ceilings, though this will be trickier to do. It's still a wonderful idea and well worth it for the pleasing effect it will create if you can manage it.

6. Wallpaper can even be used on the insides of arches or door frames.

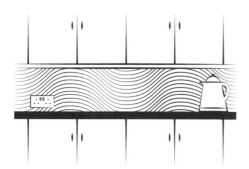

4. How about applying wallpaper to the wall above the work surface in the kitchen (if you don't have any tiles)?

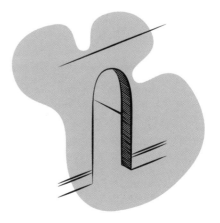

TILES

Wall tiles are most commonly found in kitchens or in the bathroom/shower room. If you're lucky, these tiles will have at least one of the following qualities: look clean, be intact, appear unassuming. Who knows, you could be in the very fortunate position of leasing a high-end or newly refurbished property.

I repeat, that's if you're lucky.

But let's get real for a second.

The majority of rental properties will go through a very long list of tenants before anything gets modernized or refreshed. Which means that permanent decorative features, such as wall tiles, for example, will probably be showing signs of wear and tear from constant use.

Or, even worse, begin to look very outdated and old-fashioned.

For a while, you'll convince yourself that you really don't mind – that you can live with a few weirdly designed tiles. But as the months pass and you are forced to gaze upon their unpleasantness day in, day out, you WILL begin to have second thoughts. In a bid to maintain your sanity, you'll finally decide that, actually, you cannot 'live like this' and swift action needs to be taken to ensure you don't have to.

Obviously, ripping these never-ever-going-to-be-called-retro tiles out and retiling is not an option here (not that you mind really, but tiling is hard work). A short-term, inexpensive fix is what you need.

Don't worry, I've got you covered.

In a bid to maintain your sanity, you'll finally decide that you cannot 'live like this' and swift action needs to be taken ... Don't worry, I've got you covered.

OPTION 1:
CLEAN AND/OR PAINT THE GROUT

This goes without saying – but regrouting? Kind of out of the question (unless the grout is so badly damaged and cracked that landlord intervention is required).

But if it's just a case of grungy or dirty-looking grout bringing down the overall appearance of the tiles, a good scrub (and/or painting the grout) may help.

Cleaning grout

You can use grout-specific cleaning products or make your own cleaning solution. I use a mixture of one part baking soda to one part vinegar: apply to the grout, then after 30 minutes use an old toothbrush to scrub it clean. Hard graft – but totally worth it.

Painting grout

If, even after cleaning, there still doesn't seem to be much improvement to the stained grouting, consider painting right over it with tile-grout paint. Fresh, white grout lines can make all the difference to the look of the tiling.

The easiest way to do this is with a grout pen, which is available in a variety of colours. This is a type of pen containing a specialized fluid that can be applied directly to grout. Each brand of pen will have different instructions for use, but, generally speaking, application is as simple as angling the pen to produce the best flow as you draw along the grout lines.

OPTION 2:
COVER THE TILES UP (YES, AGAIN WITH THE STICKY STUFF)

Out of sight, out of mind. An apt phrase if your tiles really are an eyesore. There are a few ways to do this.

Using tile stickers to cover each separate tile

These decorative stickers are made to look like actual tiles and can be applied to existing tiles (and removed) without much fuss. Most tile stickers are made from heat- and water-resistant vinyl (perfect for bathrooms), and can stand up to daily wear and tear. They can be bought from a range of online shops in a huge variety of colours and patterns. They can usually be applied to floor tiles, too.

Here is a quick guide to applying them. It is a very similar method to applying removable wallpaper but on a much smaller scale:

1. **MEASURE**
   each tile, excluding the grout lines.

2. **SELECT**
   and order your tile sticker OR make your own by cutting from a roll of self-adhesive paper.

3. **CLEAN**
   your tiles well with detergent and water.

4. **ENSURE**
   the tiles are dry with no moisture is on their surface – some bathrooms and kitchens can be quite steamy.

5. **REMOVE**
   the backing and press the sticker down on each tile and smooth out any air bubbles with your hand or a card, as before.

6. **MAKE SURE**
   you use waterproof stickers if you are intending to apply them in the bathroom – you don't want to have a build-up of mould or mildew behind them. Wait at least a day or two before exposing them to steam or water.

These stickers should easily peel off once you're ready to change the look. However, if you are having any trouble, using a hairdryer (battery powered for safety reasons if you're in the bathroom) to heat up each tile sticker before you peel it off will help. And on the rare occasion that you are left with a little glue residue, use detergent to wash the wall.

Out of sight, out of mind. An apt phrase, if your tiles really are an eyesore.

Tiling over existing tiles (mainly in the kitchen) with peel-and-stick tiles

Peel-and-stick tiles are sheets of lightweight, thin material with a self-adhesive backing that can be stuck directly to a wall. To apply them, all you have to do is measure the space, buy the right amount, peel off the backing and stick the tile sheet to the wall. A bonus is that they can be applied over existing tiles, too (although this depends on the width and depth of your grout lines, as well as the texture of the tiles). These are a fairly new product to the home-improvement market and aren't something I've tried myself. However, I thought it worth mentioning, just in case you want to do your own research on them.

Covering with panels

Alternatively, you can apply pre-cut foam, PVC or varnished wooden panels over smaller tiled areas (in particular, under kitchen cabinets) using Velcro strips or other heavy-duty adhesive strips. Paint or stencil the panels to match your décor and remove them when it's time to leave. This is something I have personally tried when styling images for photo shoots, and it does work.

Covering parts of each tile with custom self-adhesive shapes and/or decals

This works if you have a very plain, neutral-coloured expanse of tiling in need of a face-lift. Maybe you just want them stand out a little more. You can cut circles, triangles or stripes from vinyl paper, or buy ready-made wall decals/stickers to add a geometric pattern. And voila! Instant personality!

FEATURE WALLS

Feature walls (or accent walls) are a great way to make a big impact in an otherwise dull room. They are less about being subtle, and more about being playful and bold while at the same time showcasing your natural flair and style.

As this book is geared toward renters, it would be crazy for me to suggest that paint is the only way in which you can create a feature wall. Thankfully, there are many ways to achieve all the glamour of a feature wall without having to paint.

Like everything, though, there are rules – or, rather, 'guidelines'. Whether you choose to follow them or not is completely up to you…

DO

1. Put some thought into where your feature wall will be. Choosing a feature wall should have some degree of justification behind it. A shrug of your shoulders and a mumbled 'just cos' won't do, I'm afraid. Is this feature wall highlighting an existing focal point in the room such as a fireplace? If there aren't any particular features, which wall in the room is your eye naturally drawn to? That will be your focal point and so it makes sense to make this your feature wall.

2. Opt for colours in the feature wall that will complement or contrast well with the rest of the room. At the same time, though, try not to be too 'matchy matchy' with it.

DON'T

1. Put an accent wall in a tiny room. It will only make the room look smaller. You'd be far better off covering *all* the walls (especially if you've chosen a bold colour or pattern).

2. Go overboard on the furniture and accessories in a space with a feature wall. If there's too much going on, the room can just end up looking chaotic.

PROJECT #2

HOW TO APPLY ORDINARY WALLPAPER OR PAPER MURALS

Did you know that there is a way to hang wallpaper in a renter-friendly, no-damage way? Yes! Not kidding! The secret ingredient? Liquid starch. OK, granted, it only works on wallpapers that aren't already pre-pasted, but it's still awesome.

SUPPLIES

- Measuring tape and ruler
- Long-bladed scissors
- Protection for the floor
- Cloth
- Protective gloves
- Liquid starch
- Paint tray or similar container
- Foam roller
- Unpasted wallpaper or paper mural
- Wallpaper brush
- Stepladder
- Craft knife or scalpel

A few things to note:

- This is quite an ambitious project, so I would recommend trying it only if you are planning to be in your home for quite a long time and if you have a relaxed landlord (or, even better, you have your landlord's permission).
- It's always a good idea to get someone to help you apply the wallpaper, especially if you are using large pieces of wallpaper.
- If you are using wallpaper with a large pattern, be careful when cutting your strips of paper – you want to make sure the pattern will line up side-by-side when you apply the wallpaper to the wall. There's nothing worse than a lopsided, mismatched pattern.
- Remember to use the wallpaper brush to smooth out any wrinkles.

1

Measure your wall. Add at least 5–7cm
(2–3in) to each of your measurements
(you may need more if you are matching a
large pattern). Using a sharp pair of scissors,
cut lengths of wallpaper according to your
measurements.

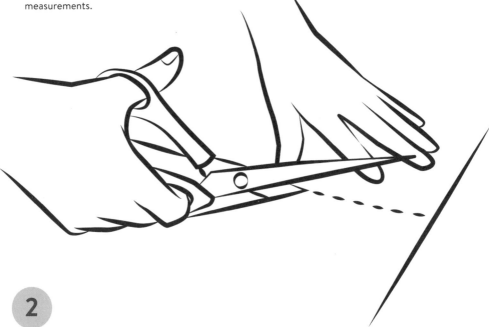

2

Place a protective covering over the floor.
Starch can be quite messy to handle and you
don't want to ruin that rented flooring.

Prepare the wall by giving it a clean with
a damp cloth and then wait for it to dry.

4

Wearing protective gloves, pour the liquid starch into the paint tray. Using a foam roller, apply the starch to the first section of wall that you'll be papering.

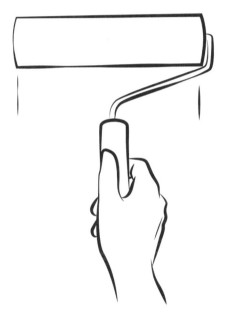

5

Hang the first piece of wallpaper from the top of the wall, leaving a little excess paper at the top. Smooth it down with a wallpaper brush so it adheres to the starch. This step can be a little tricky as the starch dries super-fast. This is where a second pair of hands is useful – and a helper can steady your stepladder if you are using one, too. Continue 'pasting' the wall and adding lengths of paper in this way. Match up any pattern and overlap seams slightly.

6

Wait until your wallpaper is completely dry, then using a ruler and a sharp craft knife, trim away the excess paper at the top, bottom and side wall edges.

AND TO REMOVE...

Simply wet the corners of the wallpaper with a damp sponge, and peel away. Use a sponge and some detergent to remove any leftover residue.

MORE FEATURE WALL IDEAS

It's not just wallpaper you can use. For the tenant whose landlord said no to painting, these ideas are for you.

REMOVABLE WALL STICKERS OR DECALS

Wall stickers are made from a very thin matt vinyl and can be used to create an all-over pattern for your wall. You can buy them ready-made in different shapes, colours and designs, or you can make your own from vinyl sticky-back plastic sheets (contact paper). Often people associate wall stickers with kids rooms but, actually, they can be used in many other settings.

Use wall stickers to create a polka-dot or triangle wall or perhaps you'd like to spell out a slogan or quote? So many options…

WASHI TAPE FEATURE WALL

Washi tape comes in lots of different widths, patterns and colours – and it is removable. No matter how long you leave it up, it doesn't damage the wall. Which makes it ideal for using to create a feature wall in a rented property. The possibilities are almost endless with washi tape. Here are a few of my favourite ideas:

- Vertical stripes
- Geometric wall design
- Crosses
- Skyline

CHALKBOARD WALL

Who doesn't like the freedom of being able to write on a wall? Best of all, you can create a complete chalkboard feature wall without all the hassle of painting (like I did!). And yes, before you ask, it will look just as good as the traditional type (and can be removed from the wall without damaging the original paint behind it).

The thing that makes this kind of feature wall renter-friendly is the specialized chalkboard sticky-back paper you will be using. To apply, follow the steps from the removable wallpaper tutorial on pages 32–5.

Once it's up, you will need to prime the paper in the same way you would with a regular chalkboard wall before you can start writing on it. You do this by rubbing the long edge of a stick of chalk lightly over the entire blackboard area. Then wipe it all off with a soft, damp cloth.

FABRIC WALL

Believe it or not, fabric can be applied to a wall just like wallpaper. Make sure to use a lightweight, cotton-type fabric, and then simply follow the steps for applying ordinary wallpaper on pages 52–53. Once done, apply another layer of starch on top of the fabric and leave to dry.

CURTAIN WALL OR TAPESTRY WALL

Nothing too fancy, but a more refined and softer way to jazz up a boring white or magnolia wall.

Install a curtain rail (or a tension rod, if you don't want to drill holes) and hang lightweight curtains or drapes that span from ceiling to floor and from wall to wall. Alternatively, you can attach a lightweight, large piece of fabric or tapestry directly to the wall using small nails, Velcro or self-adhesive hooks.

BOOKCASE FEATURE WALL

Whether you are a book lover or not, a bookcase feature wall is an excellent way to add interest to a room. It provides a fantastic backdrop for a sofa and, if you position your shelves around the TV, it can takes the focus off it while helping it to blend in. Wall-to-wall bookcases also offer a place to store other decorative items, as well as books.

Depending on how you choose to display your books (spines out or front covers out, colour-coded spines, vertical or horizontal), bookcase feature walls can also be used to add visual interest and depth to a room. And even more fun, the backing of the bookcases can be painted or wallpapered too.

You can play around with different heights of bookcase, or place sturdy blocks underneath to create extra height. Adding moulding (trim) to the fronts and sides of the bookcases where they connect with each other helps to streamline the look further.

WOODEN PLANK WALL (SHIPLAP AND OTHERS)

I'll admit that the idea of covering a wall with wood is very alarming. But hear me out – ever heard of shiplap? No? Well, it's a design feature that originated in the US and is commonly associated with the modern farmhouse style (brought back into trend by Joanna Gaines from the American TV show *The Fixer Upper*). It involves nailing plywood or MDF planks to a wall and painting them in a whitewash finish (or in some cases black). There are many different variations to it, so how you choose to install it really depends on your own style.

However, when you're renting, you might want to steer clear of any type of feature wall that involves lots of nailing. The good news is that you can buy peel-and-stick wooden planks for the wall. These are very thin wooden planks, in a variety of finishes and wood grains, with self-adhesive backing. They are more commonly found in the US and Canada, but there are a few shops in the UK that sell them. They are easy to install and can be applied to a wall in much the same way as traditional shiplap is applied – just without causing damage. Alternatively, see overleaf for a way to create and apply your own wooden planks.

PROJECT #3

INSTALLING PLANKS USING SELF-ADHESIVE STRIPS

This is a brilliantly effective way of adding interest to a room. Simply use adhesive strips to attach strips of wood across your wall. What's more, you can hammer nails into the wood so that you can hang artworks or add shelves without drilling holes into the wall itself. Result!

SUPPLIES

- Measuring tape
- Thin strips of wood
- Saw
- Paint colour of your choice (optional)
- Coloured varnish/stain (optional)
- Adhesive strips
- Spirit level
- Pencil

A few things to note:

- The only potential downside to this project is that it may end up being a little costly. Self-adhesive strips are expensive to buy and you'll need quite a few for this project.
- Adhesive strips can hold a decent amount of weight. Buy wood that is thin and lightweight (MDF, plywood or soft pine).
- Measure your wall and decide how many strips of wood you want, and how wide you want them to be. Then calculate how many strips of wood you will need. You can often get wood cut to size at larger DIY stores, or you can buy standard lengths and cut it yourself. I would suggest working with lengths of 1–1.3m (1–1½yd).
- Think of this tutorial as just the beginning. Experiment with designing your own wooden feature walls and bring them to life in your home. You could also try creating a shiplap wall (see page 51).
- If you want to make the planks or strips of wood extra-secure, and your lease allows it, you can fix them to the wall with screws, but this is not essential.

1

Once you have your strips of wood cut to size, paint them with wood paint or stain them with your choice of indoor varnish. This step needs to be done before installation as you don't want to risk getting paint or varnish on the wall. Alternatively, you may want to leave the wood bare and uncoated, in which case, simply skip this step.

2

Apply two adhesive strips to the back of each strip of wood, following the directions of the brand you are using (if you are using very long strips of wood, you may need more than two adhesive strips for each piece).

3

Starting from the bottom of your wall, use your spirit level and a pencil to draw horizontal lines so you know where to apply each strip of wood. Do not automatically assume that your walls are straight – especially in the case of older houses.

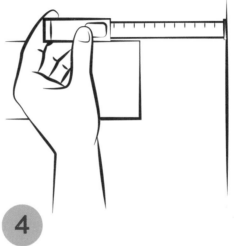

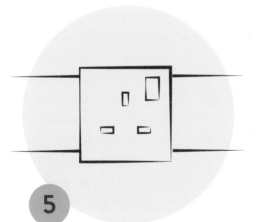

4

Starting from the left, stick your planks to the wall, following your pencil lines. Once you get near the end of the row, measure the remaining gap and cut the next strip of wood to fit.

5

For light switches or plug sockets, hold up your wood, measure the fixture and draw the dimensions onto the wood in the right place. Cut the area out of the wood using your saw.

AND TO REMOVE...

Simply follow the removal instructions for your chosen brand of adhesive strips.

FLOORING

'Um, Medina, you might want to see this.'
I looked up from the box I was unpacking to see
my husband gesturing at the floor.

We had just moved into a furnished two
bedroom property. I was in charge of unpacking
and my husband was loading some of the
unwanted furniture into the van for the landlord
to collect. First on that 'to-go' list had been the
old-fashioned green three-seater sofa.

'Look at this!' He pointed to an area on the green
(yes, green) carpet where the sofa had been.

My eyes widened when I saw it – an enormous,
dark red, shiny, but equally very matted, carpet
stain. It looked like something out of a murder
scene. It was revolting.

Of course, we hadn't noticed it before as the
stain had been cleverly hidden under the sofa.
(If this book were a novel, you could say this was
foreshadowing future events – not surprisingly,
we weren't in this property for very long.)

Ever the silver-lining seeker, my husband said
'Well, it's a good excuse to change the carpet.
I mean, it is green, after all.'

Of course, not all rented properties will have flooring that is in poor condition. Perhaps you have managed to snap up a ground-floor apartment with beautiful, stained hardwood boards? Or maybe you are renting a quirky house in the countryside with a tiled floor that has intricate features and patterns.

If that's the case (you lucky thing), some of the topics I'll be covering in this chapter won't necessarily apply to you.

I'm aware that replacing existing flooring with brand-new flooring is not always an option, especially if you're living on a short-term basis in a property, and/or don't want to splurge. So, in this chapter, I'll be sharing quick and easy tips on how to make the most of your rental flooring situation without permanently altering it or having to pull it up.

Come on, let's take a leaf out of my husband's book and find that silver lining.

DIFFERENT TYPES OF FLOORING

Before I delve into renter-friendly flooring alternatives, I thought it might be a good idea to touch on the types of flooring you might find in a rented property. I figured that if you are looking for ways to hide, enhance or even replace your flooring, it's kind of important to know what you are dealing with. Knowledge is power, after all.

CARPET

A very affordable type of flooring, carpet is commonly used in rental homes worldwide. The quality of the carpet will depend on the type and value of the property. In most cases, landlords tend to go for durable carpet in a neutral colour (beige, brown or light grey) as it wears better over time.

LINOLEUM AND VINYL

These types of flooring are most commonly found in high-traffic areas such as the kitchen, bathroom and basement. They are resilient to spills and water. While vinyl is made from PVC or plastic, lino is made from pure organic elements and does not contain any harsh chemicals, making it quite eco-friendly. Vinyl comes in a variety of styles and has a wider price and quality range – from low to premium.

LAMINATE

A much cheaper alternative to hardwood, laminate is a man-made product, engineered to look and feel exactly like hardwood. It can be bought in a variety of different lengths, thicknesses and designs.

HARDWOOD

Probably the best-looking of all the flooring options, hardwood flooring is also one of the most expensive. It is found in many high-end rented properties because of the value it adds to a house and is sometimes found in properties that were previously owner occupied. Hardwood flooring comes in a variety of forms – unfinished and pre-finished, and engineered or solid.

I'm aware that replacing existing flooring with brand-new flooring is not always an option.

TILE

Ranging from small, intricate mosaics to larger wood-effect floor tiles, this is the most versatile type of flooring in terms of materials. Porcelain and glazed ceramic tiles are the most common choices for flooring.

While tile has always been the best option for bathrooms, it can also be used in everyday dining areas, kitchens, hallways, entryways, mudrooms and laundry rooms.

CONCRETE

In the past, concrete was the ideal flooring for areas such as the basement, garage or patio. However, in recent years, it has been used in other parts of the home (such as the living room) as a sort of modern feature in either a polished or stained format. And because a concrete subfloor already exists beneath most flooring material, all that needs to be done is to remove the previous flooring to expose it, making concrete quite eco-friendly in terms of carbon footprint.

NOTE

Before we move on to renter-friendly flooring options, I should add that a new floor (even a temporary one) is something you should always discuss with your landlord first.

RUGS AND RUNNERS

Go on, admit it. You hate your rental flooring (especially the fraying carpet in the living room). You can't remember the number of times you've contemplated ripping it all up and starting over. But your negative bank balance is a constant reminder that that's not even a possibility right now – or ever. And you're fairly certain your landlord wouldn't be willing to contribute to replacement costs; he's playing the 'let's-see-how-many-years-I-can-keep-the-carpet-in-this-property-before-it-starts-to-disintegrate-completely' game.

Not a fun game for you to partake in, clearly.

Rugs are going to have to be your solution for now.

I'll expand on that, shall I?

WHY RUGS?

Rugs are incredibly stylish, and they vary in pattern, colour, texture and, most importantly, size. You can cover an entire floor from wall to wall with a good area rug. Or, similarly, add in something a little smaller if it's just to hide parts of your floor that is showing wear and tear.

I love that rugs can be shuffled around, should you suddenly become a little bored with their placement. They can also, very effortlessly, be rolled up, stored and/or taken with you to any future property.

And aside from stain coverage, rugs have other fantastic uses, too.

First, I'm a firm believer that if your room feels as if it's missing something, then you need to add a rug. A rug acts like a visual anchor and helps to bring the elements of a room together. This is particularly the case in a room that is quite large and/or open-plan and you want the different living zones to appear more defined.

And secondly, rugs help to add warmth and coziness to colder types of flooring such as hardwood, laminate or tile.

> *You're fairly certain your landlord is playing the 'let's-see-how-many-years-I-can-keep-this-old carpet-in-the-property' game. Rugs are going to have to be your solution.*

INEXPENSIVE RUG SOLUTIONS

Large rugs are expensive so no matter how tempting, you might want to resist the urge to cover every inch of your rented floor with a rug. Here are some cheaper 'rug' suggestions.

Buy flat-woven rugs

These tend to much less pricey than woven wool rugs. They will also sit better on carpet without creating a tripping hazard (good to know if you happen to be a klutz like me).

Buy second-hand/vintage

If you're comfortable with buying used textiles, you can search second-hand stores, online selling platforms or vintage shops. These rugs can always be professionally cleaned before you bring them into your home. Just be wary of carpet moths.

Layer your rugs

Layering rugs is a great way to introduce additional pattern and texture to a space. What's more, because you'll be using smaller rugs to achieve the layered look, it could be more cost-effective.

Start off with a large, neutral, flat-woven rug. Personally, I like to use a flat-weave jute or hessian type rug for the base.

Next, add a patterned or coloured rug on top, either smack in the middle or at an angle, if you want to cover a larger surface area of your floor. Just make sure that the second rug isn't too small or it will end up looking very out of place.

Carpet with bound edges

If you happen to have leftover carpet remnants from a recent flooring installation (or maybe you know someone who does), you can take them to your local carpet store and get the edges professionally bound to create a runner or a rug. Binding will give your rug straight, clean lines, and prevent it from unravelling or fraying in the future.

Carpet tiles

As far as I know, these tiles don't work so well on top of existing carpet, but they are good to go on all other flooring types. They are designed for simplicity and can be installed very quickly and easily.

PROJECT #4

MAKE YOUR OWN RUG

This is an enjoyable and super-quick way to make your own rug.

SUPPLIES

- Measuring tape
- Upholstery fabric (size and shape depends on the area you want the rug to cover)
- Anti-slip rug underlay
- Scissors
- Sewing pins
- Sewing machine
- Fabric glue (optional)

A few things to note:

- If you don't have a sewing machine, you can use fabric glue for this project instead.
- If you plan to use this rug in an area where it might be exposed to water, you can add a layer of clear glue or varnish to the surface of the fabric to seal it and make it waterproof.
- You can also use a linoleum remnant or a rubber mat for the base of the rug, if you don't have an anti-slip rug to hand. Rather than follow the steps overleaf, simply cut the fabric to size, apply it to the linoleum or rubber mat with spray adhesive and fold the fabric neatly around its edges.

1

Measure the space you intend your rug to cover, and decide how big you want the rug to be. Stick with either a square or rectangular shape.

2

Cut the fabric and the anti-slip rug underlay to your desired size, adding 5cm (2in) to both the height and the width to allow for the hem. You could use an existing rug as a template.

3

Flip the fabric over (right side down) and place the anti-slip mat on top.

4

Fold the fabric and anti-slip mat over to create a 2.5cm (1in) hem.

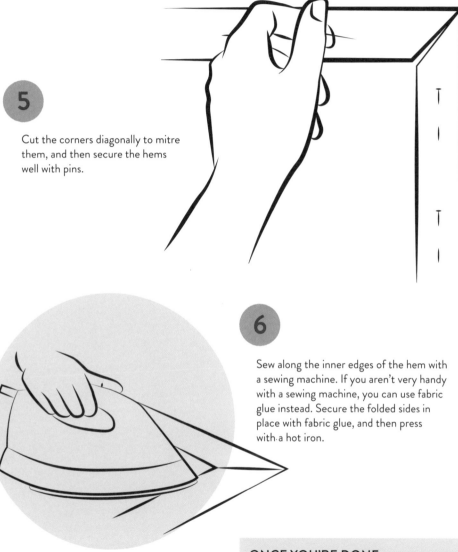

5

Cut the corners diagonally to mitre them, and then secure the hems well with pins.

6

Sew along the inner edges of the hem with a sewing machine. If you aren't very handy with a sewing machine, you can use fabric glue instead. Secure the folded sides in place with fabric glue, and then press with a hot iron.

ONCE YOU'RE DONE

Why not add some extra embellisment to your rug? You could attach small pom-poms along one side, for instance.

HOW TO TRANSFORM YOUR FLOOR

I wallpapered my floor.

Twice.

I'll admit, trying to keep a straight face while saying that is hard. I always end up smiling (or giggling) at the look of absolute shock and bewilderment on people's faces as they attempt to digest what I have just said.

Once they realize that they haven't heard me wrong, that I have indeed just said that I wallpapered my floor, then comes the barrage of quick-fire questions:

How did you do it?
Can you clean it?
Does it damage the floor when you pull it off?
What kind of wallpaper did you use?

WHY WALLPAPER A FLOOR?

Wallpapering can be a cheap and very effective solution to temporarily cover up a floor that might not be a true reflection of your style (or put bluntly, looks horrific and is in desperate needs of a facelift). This idea allows you to choose from an almost endless supply of patterns and colours to create a gorgeous floor that you will love.

Wallpaper can be applied to an array of floor types, including lino, vinyl, laminate flooring, tile and, in some cases, subflooring, provided it is flat and in good condition.

If you're still not convinced (and you should be), in the next section I will cover some other flooring options.

HOW TO WALLPAPER A FLOOR

There are two ways to wallpaper a floor (or, rather, two types of wallpaper you can use):

1. Removable wallpaper (sticky-back vinyl paper) with a self-adhesive backing
2. Traditional wallpaper

From personal experience, I can tell you that both methods work well, but the latter requires a few more steps – over the next few pages I will show you how.

To apply removable wallpaper, simply peel away the wallpaper backing and smooth it onto the floor (see pages 34–5). Once the paper is in place, follow steps 5–7 on page 75. To remove, simply peel away at a corner – try applying a little heat with a hairdryer, if the wallpaper is a bit stubborn.

71

PROJECT #5

HOW TO APPLY TRADITIONAL WALLPAPER TO A FLOOR

Hopefully, I've managed to convince you that wallpapering your floor is the way forward, and this tutorial will show you how. It works on wooden floors, laminate, lino, vinyl and tiled floors.

SUPPLIES

- Wallpaper
- Measuring tape
- Scissors
- PVA glue
- Roller or paintbrush
- Damp cloth or card
- Craft knife or scalpel
- Sandpaper 180–220 grit (optional)
- Clear floor varnish (polyurethane)
- Paint-stirring stick
- Paint tray
- Wool floor applicator

A few things to note:

- I wouldn't really advise this floor treatment for rooms that have a large surface area to cover. The smaller, the better – think utility room, toilet, bathroom, porch (foyer).
- You can wallpaper over a hard flooring with grooves (such as laminate, for example), but those grooves shouldn't be more than 5mm (¼in) wide or the wallpaper will just sink into the grooves and tear (especially if you happen to be wearing heels).
- Ensure the flooring surface is flat and smooth before applying the wallpaper. Sand down wooden floors or fill in any imperfections with wood filler if need be.
- Always sweep the floor to remove any loose debris. Then clean it with detergent and water and leave to dry, before starting to apply the wallpaper.

1

Roll out your first piece of wallpaper on the floor and cut to size, leaving at least 5cm (2in) extra at each end. Repeat with the next piece, carefully matching the pattern at the sides, and continue in this way until the floor is covered. This will enable you to ensure you have enough paper before you start sticking everything down.

2

3

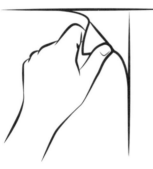

Remove the pieces in order (numbering them on the back, if pattern-matching has been tricky). Starting in one corner, take the first piece and place it down. Lift one end of the wallpaper up, and apply the glue adhesive with a roller or paintbrush to either the back of the paper or the floor. Press down and smooth firmly. Keep doing this in stages until the first piece of paper is completely adhered to the floor.

Apply the next piece of paper, taking your time to make sure it lines up exactly with the first piece (particularly if you are using a patterned design). Don't overlap the edges but try to get the pieces as close together as possible. For now, don't worry about the excess paper at the wall edges.

4

Continue laying your pieces of wallpaper, smoothing out any wrinkles or air bubbles with the damp cloth or card. Avoid stepping on the paper you have already laid as it will move and wrinkle underfoot when wet. Once the floor is covered, leave it to dry overnight.

5

Once dry, use your knife to remove the excess wallpaper. Neaten up the corners and edges around the skirting boards (baseboards). As long as you are using a sharp blade, the paper should cut away quite easily.

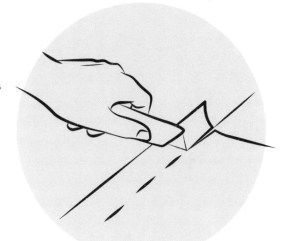

6

Optional, but you can also give the whole floor a light sanding with 180–220 grit paper before applying a sealant, to help the varnish soak in. Just be sure to sweep or vaccum up any resulting dust.

7

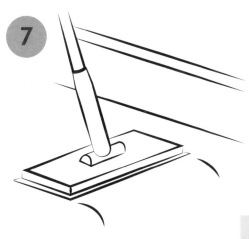

Finally, the floor needs to be sealed. Open a can of clear, non-yellowing varnish (polyurethane), stir well and then pour into a paint tray. For best results, use a wool floor applicator or a floor pad with a handle and apply the varnish to the floor in long, even strokes – this way you won't walk on the varnish as you apply it. You will need at least three coats. Leave the floor to dry between coats, according to the product instructions. Once the final coat is done, do not walk on the floor for at least 12 hours.

AND TO REMOVE...

Simply peel off a corner and pull away. Scrub the existing floor with detergent and water to remove any paper or glue residue.

PROJECT #6

HOW TO PAINT A FLOOR

In all honesty, you can paint almost anything. And that includes most types of traditional flooring materials. But just because you can paint anything, doesn't necessarily mean you should.

SUPPLIES

- Orbital sanding machine (optional) with dust masks
- Sandpaper, 180–220 grit
- Floor cleaning solution
- Painter's tape
- Floor primer
- Foam rollers (preferably with long handle extensions)
- Paint tray
- Floor paint (in the colour of your choice)
- Paint-stirring stick

A few things to note:

- Remember, you will need to get your landlord's approval before painting any floor in your home.
- Painting a floor requires a lot of time and preparation. In other words, the decision to paint a floor shouldn't be taken lightly. While it is a very simple (and easy, depending on how you look at it) way to give an ugly floor a make-over, it does need to be done correctly. You don't want the paint scraping off at the lightest of touches a few weeks down the line. So my best advice? Take your time and don't rush any of these steps.
- The following tutorial is a generic one and can therefore be used for all types of flooring as the general principles will remain the same.
- You could paint stripes or a pattern onto the floor, if you're feeling a bit more adventurous. You'll just need to apply painter's tape to the floor in the shape of your pattern before painting – when you peel it away, the pattern will be revealed.
- It's advisable to use specific floor paint for this as it'll be more resistant to the wear and tear of everyday foot traffic. The two types are oil based or latex enamel, and they come in gloss or matt finishes. If you aren't using a floor-specific paint, you will need to seal the floor with clear varnish (polyurethane) to protect it once the paint is dry.

1

Sanding is a must, especially if you are painting a hardwood or laminate floor. You will need to remove the top layer of flooring to give the primer something to adhere to. It will also help to smooth out any lumps or bumps. If you have a large surface area to cover, renting an orbital sander is a good idea (always make sure you wear a protective dust mask when sanding). If you are painting vinyl or tile, a light sanding by hand with 180–220 grit sandpaper will be enough. Once sanded, vacuum or brush up the dust.

2

If painting hardwood flooring, make sure to give it a good sweep. For all other types of flooring, cleaning is important. Using a specific floor-cleaning solution will help to lift the dirt and dust from the floor. Once cleaned, leave the floor to dry naturally.

3

If you plan on painting stripes or any other design, now is the time to roll out the painter's tape. Also, don't forget to protect your skirting boards (baseboards) and door frames with tape as well.

4

Now you need to prime your floor. Use a good-quality primer, especially on flooring that previously had a glossy surface such as laminate or tile. To test, apply the primer to a small patch of floor. Once dry, scrape at it with your nails. If the primer instantly comes off, you'll know it's not going to do the job; if it doesn't scrape off, you can do a little happy dance, because you have yourself a good primer. To apply the primer, either pour it directly onto the floor from the can and then roll it out with the foam roller, or pour it into a tray, roll it onto the roller and then the floor. If you are painting tiled flooring, you will need to ensure the primer covers the grout lines. Leave the primer to dry overnight (but, again, always follow the specific manufacturer's instructions for drying times).

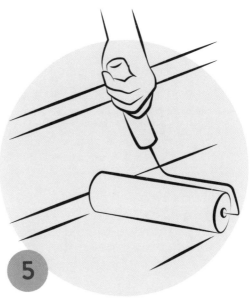

5

When your primer is dry, you can finally paint the top coat. Stir the paint well before using, and then paint the floor in the same way that you applied the primer. If you need a second coat, leave enough time between coats for the paint to fully dry.

6

In cases where you aren't using a floor-specific paint, you will now need to seal the floor with varnish to protect it.

7

Do not place anything on the floor or walk on it until it has completely dried.

STAIRS

Because stairs are often seen only for their functional purpose and rarely for their aesthetic potential, they are usually the last place in a house that people will think to decorate.

This is bizarre, really, when you think about it, because in many cases the stairs are the first thing someone will see when they walk into a house, whether that be in the entrance hall or in the main, open-plan living space in which they form a design feature.

And we all know first impressions count for everything, right?

So why not make that first impression memorable by beautifying your staircase. If you've been playing it safe with the rest of the house, now is the time to throw caution to the wind (well, OK, don't throw it away completely, I don't want you to lose your deposit) and be super-inventive.

While you won't be able to alter the physical structure of the staircase itself (renter perks and all), you can certainly make each step pop by adding statement features of your own.

You can certainly make each step pop by adding statement features of your own.

HOW TO IMPROVE YOUR STAIRS

OPTION 1: RECARPETING

I know. This sounds perfectly mundane. But hear me out. If your current stairs are either carpeted with a material that looks the worse for wear, or without carpet, and the exposed material is in really bad condition, laying a fresh, new carpet will make the world of difference.

But remember, you will need to get your landlord's approval. And bear in mind that changing the stair carpet will often mean replacing the top landing carpet as well.

Oh, wait, was that a dollar sign that just flashed before your eyes? You guessed it. Expensive. But, hey, if the carpet on the stairs was really damaged when you moved in, then you could put a case to your landlord asking him/her to contribute to the costs.

If you aren't willing to go down this route, you could try:

Just carpeting the stair treads

With this method, only the stair treads are covered with carpet, which is stapled in place, while the risers are left bare.

You might get a very confused look from the carpet fitter as you attempt to explain your vision, but most will be able to install it this way (for an extra cost, I must add, since it will take more time). The resulting effect is fantastic and well worth it, though. You get all the benefits of a carpet, along with the added bonus of being able to add character to the step risers.

TIP: you can also buy pre-cut carpet treads online to achieve a similar look.

Add a patterned runner

Preferably using Velcro or a staple gun, if the landlord approves. A quick search online for 'stunning staircase runners' will show you the transformative effect a gorgeous runner can have and will provide you with plenty of inspiration.

 Was that a dollar sign that just flashed before your eyes? You guessed it. Expensive.

OPTION 2 : REMOVING CARPET (IF PRESENT) AND REFINISHING THE WOOD

The original staircase wood needs to be in fairly good condition for you to be able to do this.

This process involves:

1. Filling in any holes or dents in the wood with natural wood filler.

2. Sanding each step and riser with a heavy-duty sander to smooth the surface and remove any previous paint or varnish.

3. Applying wood stain (in your choice of colour) and finishing off with the appropriate floor varnish. Although, it should be said, you don't necessarily need to stain it. You can leave the wood bare, if you like the raw, exposed look, and just varnish the wood to protect it.

OPTION 3: REMOVING CARPET (IF PRESENT) AND PAINTING THE STAIRS

This process involves:

1. Filling in any holes or dents in the wood with natural wood filler.

2. Sanding each step and riser with a heavy-duty sander to smooth the surface and remove any previous paint or varnish.

3. Applying a very good-quality primer to the staircase.

4. Applying a top coat (or two) of floor paint.

OPTION 4: A COMBINATION OF REFINISHING AND PAINTING

You could try mixing it up with painted risers combined with stained or exposed treads. You can mix and match paint colours and stains of your choosing.

All four of the above options form the groundwork for even more exciting staircase decorating possibilities. Here some more ideas to improve your stairs.

WALLPAPERED STEPS

I would suggest using removable wallpaper or sticky-back vinyl for this method, simply because it is easier. Although traditional wallpaper can be used (much in the same way as I described in wallpapering a floor on pages 72–5), this process is a lot messier and a little more time consuming. If you do opt to use traditional wallpaper, it needs to be the unpasted kind and should be applied to the stairs with PVA glue, not wallpaper paste (which will leave lasting damage to the surface).

Tips for applying removable wallpaper to stair risers:

- When choosing your wallpaper, go for something with an eye-catching pattern that will complement the space it's in. If you are uncertain, order a few samples before committing.

- Make sure you measure each stair riser individually – don't assume each one is the same, especially in older houses where features are often not symmetrical or straight. Once you've measured, you will be able to estimate how many panels of removable paper you will need.

- Trim each panel to size using either a craft knife and cutting mat or a pair of sharp scissors for nice, crisp lines.

- Peel off the backing from one end of the panel and apply it to the edge of the riser, easing the backing off and sticking a little at a time, working from one side of the stairs to the other. Smooth out any bubbles as you go.

ANYTHING PAINT CAN DO, REMOVABLE PRODUCTS CAN

Did you just sing that out loud? I know I did! Here are just a few examples:

- **Racing stripes staircase:** apply rolls of varying widths of sticky vinyl paper down one side of the staircase for this classic look.

- **Faux-painted risers:** apply solid coloured panels (cut from a roll of contact paper) to each stair riser.

- **Chalkboard risers:** apply chalkboard paper to each stair riser and scribble a design on each one.

- **Numbered steps:** arrange number stickers in order and apply them to the centre or corners of each stair riser for an industrial feel.

- **Faux-painted mural risers:** cut a removable, wallpaper mural into appropriately sized strips and apply them to your risers.

- **Marble- or wood-effect risers:** you can buy removable wallpaper with marble or wood effects and apply them to your risers OR use peel-and-stick wooden slats.

- **Exotic tile stairs:** use tile stickers or peel-and-stick mosaic tiles.

I could go on, but I'd be here all day…

STORAGE

Husband: 'Any reason why we're now storing nappies in the kitchen drawer?'

Me: 'I don't know. Does the fact we no longer have a spare room count as a reason?'

Husband: 'It doesn't. You can still store stuff in there.'

Me: 'Can I? Our son's cot is the size of the bedroom itself. There is absolutely NOWHERE to store anything in there – and don't say under the cot because his pushchair is already there.'

Surprisingly, my husband didn't call me out. He just agreed. At first. But then again, it was 2012. And that was the year of many firsts.

It was the year our son was born (also known as 'the year we didn't sleep').

It was the year we promised to adult better, to give up our reckless serial-renter ways and settle down. (Spoiler: we broke that promise.)

It was the year we found ourselves, for the first time, at the mercy of a landlord who would not agree to any kind of decorating (holes to put up shelves for storage were out of the question)

It was also the year that the second bedroom (which in our previous homes had always functioned as a dumping ground, of sorts, to appease my hoarding habits) became a nursery. And, hence, the year that storage suddenly became a huge problem.

Two adults and a baby in a two-bedroom ground-floor flat – sounds ideal when you say it out loud, doesn't it? In reality, though, it was anything but. Here's why:

- The flat, in true British style, was quite compact.

- The kon-mari method made famous by Marie Kondo was not yet known in the UK and we had far too much unnecessary clutter.

- Our landlord was a major control freak.

- As for our son – who knew such small beings came with so many (large) gadgets and (even larger) must-have accessories?

In this chapter, I'll be showing you how to maximize the space you do have to create a home that feels welcoming and spacious. I'll also be sharing some simple and affordable storage tips. There are a few projects that involve a little DIY (and maybe the odd power tool), but please don't be put off. I've kept everything at beginner level, and have even thrown in some alternate methods for that level before 'beginner'.

STORAGE TIPS FOR RENTERS

Living in a small space without really wanting to adopt a minimalist lifestyle can be challenging. Even more so when it's a rented property and you are limited by the number of changes you're allowed to make. But are there any simple storage ideas that can be adopted by renters to make life a little easier? Yes!

DECLUTTER

One of the positive things about renting (especially if you happen to be the type who moves around a lot) is that there will be plenty of opportunities to look around your home and think, 'Do I really need all this?'

That day is usually moving day. Or the few days before moving day, when you are frantically packing up the contents of your life into cardboard boxes. As you bubble-wrap glass, china and precious homeware, you'll find yourself wondering just how you've accumulated so much stuff over the years.

Do you really need that coffee machine with the missing button? The tangled cluster of computer wires? Or the 17 odd socks that no longer have a partner?

That day (or, ideally, slightly before) is the time to start decluttering. Think of it as a house detox before a fresh new start. Figuring out what needs to go is a tough process, but once you do, make a donation to your local charity.

Alternatively, try selling some of your items online – although I must warn you, the promise of quick money transfers might

sound appealing but the process is not. Selling online can be time-consuming and infuriating. No matter how clearly you describe the items you want to sell, you'll get plenty of questions such as 'How much is this?' and 'What are the dimensions?'

'Give me strength!', you'll want to scream.

BUY MULTIFUNCTIONAL FURNITURE

Multifunctional furniture provides a way to get more utility from a space. Great examples are:

- Beds with additional storage underneath

- A stylish ottoman that can function as both a coffee table and a place for storing blankets

- A table that can be folded down into a desk or extended for entertaining guests.

- Chairs that can be folded when not in use and either hung or stacked elsewhere

- Bench seating with cubbyholes or space underneath for baskets to store toys, magazines or other small items

SWAP OUT BULKY FURNITURE

Bulky furniture such as dressers, wardrobes and nightstands, can take up a lot of wall space (not to mention, make a room look and feel smaller). They all have an important role to play within a room (especially the bedroom), so I'm not suggesting you get rid of them completely. Instead, opt for leaner versions or think about storage ideas that serve the same purpose but take up much less space. This will allow the flow of natural light and create a roomier feel.

Examples include:

- A clothes rack or rail as opposed to a full wardrobe

- Stools, piles of books/magazines or slim shelves instead of nightstands

- Wooden ladders used to hang blankets and throws

VIEW ALL SPACES AS A POTENTIAL FOR STORAGE

Think beyond the primary functions or features of items in your home – fixtures can often serve more than one purpose.

Take a door, for example. Thinking outside the box, a door, whether it be of a cupboard, wardrobe or entrance, can also be used as a means for storage. Products such as over-door shoe holders, over-door peg rails/hooks, self-adhesives hooks, baskets or pantry racks can all be secured to a door (without drilling I must add) and used to organize various household items.

It's important to keep an open mind about how you utilize things. For example, a plastic shoe rack can be used to store items other than shoes, including toys, jewellery, tools or household cleaning products.

There are lots of spots in the house that can provide extra storage that you might have overlooked, for example:

1. **Window sills:** these are, in essence, handy built-in shelves so why not treat them as such? You can use them to display books, magazines, plants and so on. Just don't forget to add a bookend to keep your books upright.

2. **Above doors or windows**: add wall shelving. Most people won't bother to look up when they walk into a room, so this is the perfect place to 'conceal' items that you don't need every day.

5. **Underneath wall cabinets:** add sliding wire baskets on racks under cabinets or shelves.

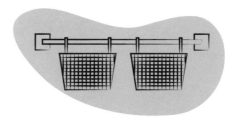

3. **Under the stairs:** this compact space can be transformed into a functional living zone, or it can be used for extra storage. Simply measure the space and add in bookcases, shelves or even a desk of the appropriate size.

6. **Under the bed:** opt for beds with built-in drawers or use under-bed boxes/baskets on wheels for storage.

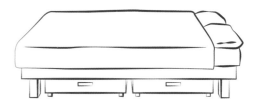

Which brings me to our first DIY idea of the chapter…

4. **Corners and alcoves:** while you won't be able to install custom-built cabinets without your landlord's permission, you can add bookcases, narrow tables or cabinets with additional shelving on top.

PROJECT #7

HOW TO BUILD UNDER-BED STORAGE BOXES

These rolling under-bed storage boxes are the perfect space-saving solution for toys, shoes, blankets, sheets, books and out-of-season clothes. If you already have large boxes or drawers, you can skip the first few steps and head straight to step 8, adding the wheels part.

SUPPLIES

To build one box:
- Softwood planks, 18mm (¾in) thick, cut to your desired length
- Drill
- Wood glue
- 30–40 screws, 40mm (1½in) long
- Screwdriver
- Plywood sheet, 9mm (⅜in thick)
- Electric jigsaw or handsaw
- 4 small castor wheels
- 16 screws for castors, 10mm (⅜in) long
- Heavy duty adhesive (optional)
- 1 knob or pull for box front
- Tape measure
- Washi tape, wallpaper or paint, to decorate

A few things to note:

- Before you buy your supplies, make sure you measure the width and height of the space under your bed and jot down the dimensions. Work out how big you need the box(es) to be, remembering to allow for the height of the castor wheels.

- For perfectly square boxes, remember to take in to account the thickness of the planks – two planks will need to be 36mm (1½in) shorter than the other two.

- I would advise getting your wood and plywood cut to size (you can often do this at larger DIY stores). Otherwise, buy standard lengths and cut it yourself using an electric jigsaw or handsaw – just try and make your cuts as straight as possible.

- Be inventive when it comes to decorating your storage boxes. They might not be the first thing you see when you go into your bedroom, but that doesn't mean you can't make them look fun and stylish. Use paint, washi tape or leftover scraps of wallpaper to create bold geometric patterns or add a splash of colour. You could even use stencils to make more intricate designs.

1

With a drill bit of the appropriate size for the diameter of your long screw, mark and drill two holes at each end of the longer planks. These holes will be used to attach the end of one of the shorter planks (see next step), so make sure the holes are evenly spaced and near to the edge of the plank.

2

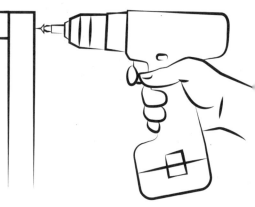

Assemble the first corner of the box. Apply glue to the end of the shorter plank. Stick the pieces of wood together at a right angle and secure in place with two screws through the holes you made in the previous step.

3

Repeat steps 1 and 2 for the other three corners until you have a complete box.

4

If your plywood has not yet been cut to size, use the assembled sides of your box to draw the outline onto the plywood sheet. Align two of the edges to save cutting time. Use the jigsaw or handsaw to cut the base to size.

5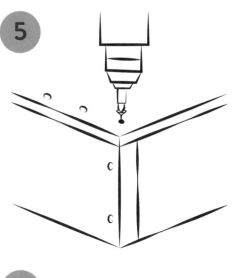

Lay the base in position and drill holes for the screws at regular intervals (around 6–7 along each edge, depending on the size of your box). Screw base down.

6

Screw a castor wheel to each corner of the base. If you don't want to use screws here, a heavy duty adhesive is a good alternative.

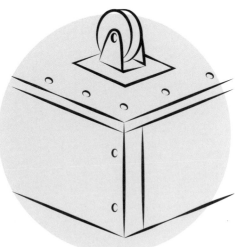

7

Attach a knob or pull. Using your tape measure, find the centre of the front of your box, mark it with a pencil and then drill a hole (or two) as required to fix your knob in place.

8

Decorate your box with paint, washi tape or leftover scraps of wallpaper.

PROJECT #8

DIY CRATE SHELVING

This is probably obvious, but if floor space is limited, the only way to expand on storage capabilities is by going up. And that doesn't necessarily have to involve drilling holes or putting up huge shelving contraptions.

Wooden crates are a fantastic (and fairly cheap) way to create storage. Simply recycle old wooden crates and stack them on top of each other to create storage for various miscellaneous items including books, clothing, shoes and so on. What's even better than stacked crate storage? Stacked crate storage on wheels!

SUPPLIES

- 2 crates
- Sandpaper (optional)
- Clear polyutherane varnish (optional)
- 6 screws, 25mm (1in) long
- Screwdriver
- Wood glue or heavy duty adhesive (optional)
- 16 screws for castors, 10mm (⅜in) long
- 4 small castor wheels
- Wallpaper for decoration (optional)

A few things to note:

- If you would prefer not to use a screwdriver, these crates can be stacked using wood glue or heavy duty adhesive (but note that this method is not reversible, so you won't be able to unstack the crates in the future).
- Once you've created your crate shelving, play around with decoration. Try adding removable wallpaper to the back of each create, or paint them a bright colour.
- These shelves will work anywhere in the home. They can hold your magazine collection in the living room, serve as a bedside table, or house your bathroom toiletries. As the shelves are on wheels, you can move them around as you fancy.

1

If you are recycling old wooden crates, it's a good idea to sand them first. Sand the wood well, smoothing any rough edges, and clean up any loose debris. This may take some time but it's worth it. Dust them off once completed. You could also paint the crates with clear polyutherane varnish to seal the wood and give it a protective coating.

2

Decide how you would like to arrange your crates. I stacked rectangular crates on their long sides.

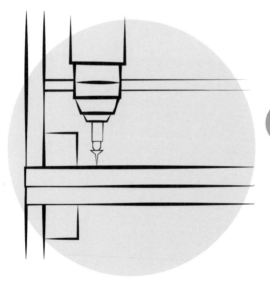

3

Secure the top crate to the bottom crate using the 25mm (1in) long screws. It shouldn't be necessary to drill holes first. Alternatively, you can use wood glue or heavy duty adhesive to fix the crates together – but this method is not reversible, so you won't be able to unstack the crates in the future.

4

Attach the castor wheels to the corners of the underside of the bottom crate. Ensure the screws aren't too long and won't pierce through the crate 'floor'.

5

This is optional, but if you want to give your storage a decorative touch, try adding removable wallpaper or other decorative paper to the inside back wall of each wooden crate.

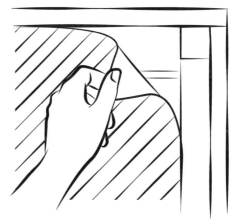

WALL SHELVING

Wall shelving is a great way to tidy away clutter. It's also a great way to organize and display items that reflect your personal style. Think stylish shelfies.

But is there a way to install a wall shelf without making holes? To be honest, not really. And that's especially the case if you want a shelf that is able to hold a decent amount of weight.

If your shelf will only be used for lightweight decorative items, then heavy-duty adhesive strips can be used to suspend hanging shelving.

However, if sturdy weight-bearing wall shelves are the direction you want to take, you will need to run it by your landlord first. The installation is going to involve holes and wall plugs at the very least. And you might want to do a quick crash course on how to fill in holes without bodging the walls (holes don't count as normal wear and tear and will have to be filled in before you leave).

There are many different types and styles of wall shelving available. My advice is to stick with the kind that requires the least amount of drilling. Which pretty much takes floating shelves out of the equation. They require about a zillion screws to keep them afloat and are just an all-round pain to put up (in my opinion).

Here are some other examples of wall shelving you can buy that won't require too much hole-making:

- Picture ledges
- Pegboard shelving (this can also be leaned up against a wall)
- Twin-slot bracket shelving
- Box shelving
- Shelves hung from cup hooks with rope

You might want to do a quick crash course on how to fill in holes without bodging the walls.

DIY LEAN-AGAINST-THE-WALL SHELVES

This project is perfect if you want to display a few books, pictures and plants without making a lot of holes in the wall. The beauty of the leaning shelf is that it requires only one screw into the wall (and that is purely for safety reasons).

SUPPLIES

- Structural plywood, half a standard sheet, 2440 x 610 x 18mm (96 x 24 x ¾in), with three 'shelves' cut from one end to the depth of your choice
- Sandpaper or sanding machine and mask
- Tape measure
- Pencil
- Drill
- Wood glue
- 12 screws, 40mm (1½in) long
- Screwdriver
- Screw hook and screw eye
- Wall plug (optional)

A few things to note:

- The shelves are attached to the back board with screws, so they won't be strong enough to hold a lot of very heavy books, but will be sturdy enough to hold a mixture of books and lighter items.
- Structural plywood is very solid and won't warp, but as it's thick and heavy, it's best to get it cut to size at the place where you buy it. Many DIY stores offer this service for free and their machines will give a perfectly straight, smooth cut every time.

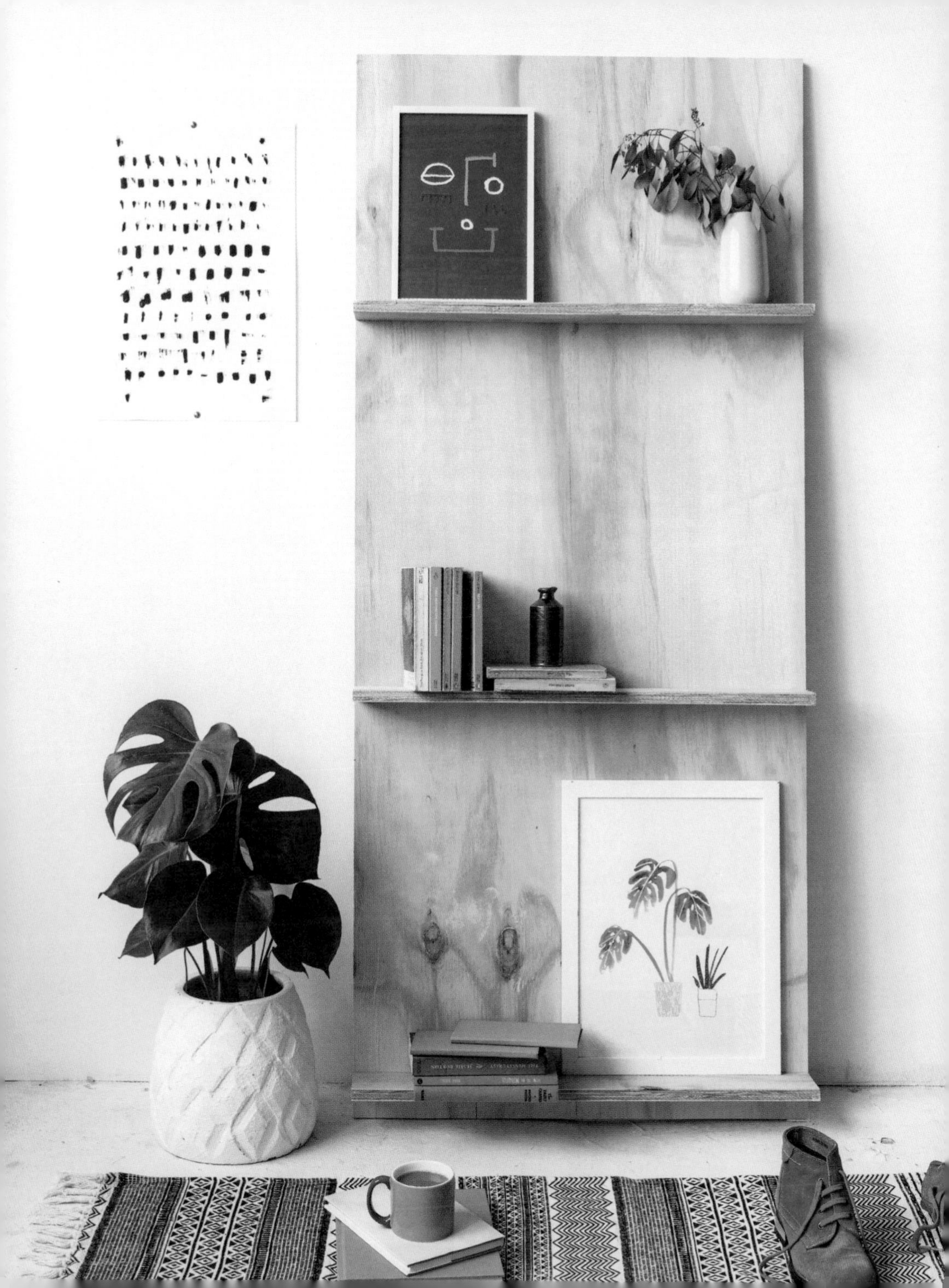

1

Give the cut plywood pieces a light sanding with sandpaper (or your sander). Pay particular attention to the sides and edges.

2

Lay the backing board face down on the floor (protect the floor if necessary). Decide exactly where you want the shelves to go on your backing board, using the tape measure to space them evenly apart. Once your placement is set, mark a line across the backing board where the centre of each shelf will sit.

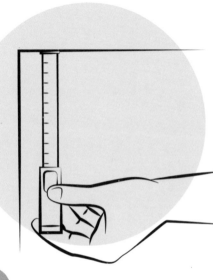

3

Mark three evenly spaced intervals along each 'shelf line' where the screws will attach the shelves to the backing board.

4

Using a drill bit that's a size smaller than your screw diameter, drill holes in the backing board along your pencil lines. If in doubt, always use the smaller drill bit as you can easily enlarge the hole, if necessary; you can't, however, make it smaller.

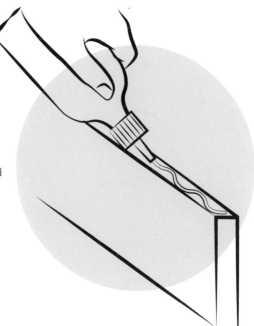

5

Flip the backing board over so that the markings are on the underside. Apply wood glue to the back edge of the first shelf and position it centrally over the drilled holes. You need the screws to go into the middle of the shelf, not to poke out at the top or bottom. Press it firmly in place, then repeat for the other shelves.

6

Once the glue is dry, carefully turn the whole piece over, so it is resting on the shelf fronts. Secure each shelf with screws through the drilled holes.

7

Screw the eye screw to the top centre of the shelf unit on the back. Lean the unit in place, and screw the corresponding hook screw into the wall – you may need to drill the wall and use wall plugs.

PROJECT #10

DIY PEGBOARD

This board is great for storing a wide range of items within your home. It can be propped up on furniture or the floor, if you don't want to attach it to the wall. This project shows how to create the base pegboard.

A few things to note:

- The brilliant thing about this pegboard is that the configuration of pegs and dowels is never fixed. So play around with your home accessories, see which combinations work best and then display them in any way you want. The options are limitless.
- As I mentioned earlier, structural plywood is thick and heavy, so it's best to get it cut to size at the place where you buy it. Many DIY stores offer this service for free and their machines will give a perfectly straight, smooth cut every time.
- And if you want to put shelves on top of some of the pegs (as I have done here), ask to have some extra pieces of plywood cut to the size you want your shelves to be. Looping a small rubber band around the dowels can help shelves to stay put, or they can be glued in place for more security.

1 Place your sheet of plywood on two stands or some sturdy blocks so it is off the floor. The drill will go right through the sheet so you need to ensure the floor underneath is not in danger of being damaged.

2 Figure out your spacing. I went with a 10cm (4in) grid, drawing vertical lines at 10cm (4in) intervals and then horizontal lines at 10cm (4in) intervals.

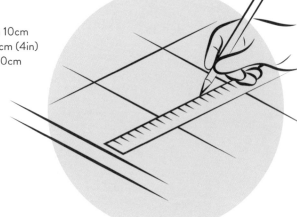

3 Measure and mark your grid lightly with a pencil (you will need to remove the marks later).

4

Each intersection of lines on your grid is where your pegs will go. To keep hole placement accurate and prevent the wood from cracking, drill pilot holes with a small drill bit where the lines cross first.

5

Swap the small drill bit for the 22mm (⅞in) one. Carefully drill into each hole, ensuring that you keep your drill at a 90-degree angle to the board.

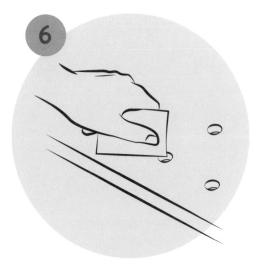

7

Push some dowels in and try out different configurations. If you are cutting your own dowels to length, figure out how long you want them, cut one as a test, make any adjustments, then cut as many as you need.

6

Give all the holes a light sanding with sandpaper. Remove any pencil marks with an eraser or sandpaper.

PROJECT #11

DIY CLOTHES RACK

A DIY clothes rack is a great place to hang clothes. With storage underneath, you will be able to free up some space in your closet (or this can be the closet).

A few things to note:

- Those of you who like to shove as many clothes as possible into your wardrobe, force the doors closed and then run away, this is probably not for you. However, for the tidy people among you, this project is a brilliant way of displaying your favourite items of clothing, and bringing colour into a bare room.
- Again, as I mentioned earlier, structural plywood is thick and heavy, so it's best to get it cut to size when you buy it. Many DIY stores offer this service for free and their machines will give a perfectly straight, smooth cut every time. You will need two 120 x 40cm (48 x 16in) pieces and two 30 x 40cm (12 x 16in) pieces.

1

Assemble the pieces of wood to form a rectangular box (with a front and back that is open). See page 96, steps 1–3, for how to assemble the pieces. In this instance, the two narrow side panels should sit inside the ends of the larger rectangular top and bottom pieces.

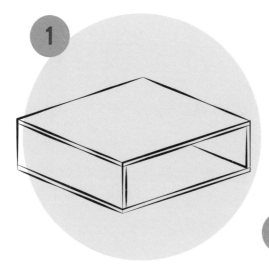

2

Once the glue has fully dried, sand the entire base with a sanding machine.

3

Attach a castor wheel to each corner of the bottom of the base using 16mm (⅝in) screws.

4

Assemble the clothes rail: screw a long pipe into one of the flanges, then screw an elbow corner to the top.

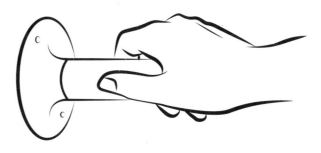

5

Screw the shorter pipe into the other side of the elbow corner, and screw the remaining elbow corner onto the end of it. Finally, screw the second longer pipe onto the elbow corner to create a U-shaped rail, and add the second flange to the end.

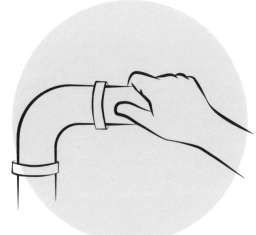

6

Screw the rail to the top of the wooden base through the holes in the flanges, ensuring they are placed so that the rail is central.

OTHER STORAGE IDEAS

And to round off this chapter, here are even more ideas for maximizing storage in your home.

BASKETS ARE YOUR BEST FRIENDS

No kidding, here's why:

- They are great for hiding (or organizing) clutter, including toys, books, shoes, clothes or any small items.
- They look great while hiding said clutter and you can buy them in all different shapes, sizes and styles to suit your needs.
- They add texture to bland spaces – and you'll need a little more depth if your walls are magnolia.
- They can be placed inside larger pieces of furniture to create a more streamlined, organized look.
- They are affordable (for the most part).
- They can be labelled (handy if you live with someone who struggles to find things that are right under his or her nose).

HOOKS ARE ALSO BEST-FRIEND MATERIAL

Hooks are a great way to organize things in any room. They can be used in the bathroom for clothes and towels, or in the kitchen for mugs, utensils or dishcloths and so on.

There are many types of adhesive hooks on the market that can be attached to walls or doors without requiring any permanent alterations. They can easily be applied and removed when needed, and you'll be surprised at just how much weight they can hold.

INTRODUCE ADDITIONAL STORAGE SYSTEMS TO CUPBOARDS/ WARDROBES

Make the most of the space in any large cabinets, closets or wardrobes that your rented home already has. Add in extra baskets, rails, hooks to the backs of the doors or even slim chests of drawers. Take the word maximizing to a whole new level.

CREATE YOUR OWN UTENSIL HOLDER

If your kitchen utensils are lacking a home, don't just stash them in a drawer. Screw some pipe clips into a piece of wood (painted or varnished), then add some adhesive strips to the back and fix to the wall. Done!

LIGHTING
AND
WINDOWS

'The Eighties called, they want their curtains back!' – I joked as I watched my husband remove the heavy, lined curtains from our tiny kitchen window.

He laughed. 'Aren't you an Eighties kid?'

He pulled a face as he threw the curtains into a trash bag I was holding. 'Ugh, these stink!'

'They really do,' I agreed, scrunching up my nose in disgust.

This house was full of surprises and the kitchen, in particular, was dreadful. The natural lighting wasn't great, for a start. There was only one window, which was really small and faced a brick alleyway (not much of a view).

And then there was the lighting. There was only one pendant light positioned toward the end of the room, which didn't help much as the kitchen was quite long and narrow.

We had to do something about it, but within reason of course. You know that emoji with one drop of sweat? Kind of apt here.

Light fixtures and windows are both examples of those built-in features that landlords prefer to keep on the more practical and durable side. Expect to see wall-flush lights, pendant lights that aren't centred, outdated net curtains, light switches that are in the wrong position and so forth. Believe me, I've seen it all.

But good lighting is so important, and there is absolutely no reason why you should live without it, in darkness.

In this chapter, I'll show you tips and hacks that will enable you to make the most of the lighting in your property. All very budget-friendly and easy, of course, and nothing that will ever involve you having to figure out how to rewire your switches, I promise.

THE IMPORTANCE OF GOOD LIGHTING

Good lighting is so important because it:

- Sets the mood in a room. Apparently, brighter lights are used in the workplace because it boosts productivity, so just imagine what the right lighting will do for us in our homes.

- Has the potential to create a warm and inviting ambiance.

- Creates visual interest by emphasizing wall paints, floors and other accessories in your home.

- Adds depth and dimension to a room. Sometimes it can make a space seem much bigger than it is.

Bad lighting is the opposite of the above.

THE FOUR KINDS OF LIGHTING

A room should have four types of lighting. An awareness of each of them will help you to address any lighting issues you might face in your rented property.

1. NATURAL LIGHT

Natural light is very important. However, if you rent, you won't always have much say in the design of the features that allow sunlight into your home, namely, the windows. Consequently, it's a good idea to look for other ways to compensate for a lack of natural sunlight. For example:

- Place mirrors on the walls opposite the windows, so that they reflect daylight and create a brighter home.

- Avoid heavy, dark window treatments such as very thick, fully lined curtains.

- Steer clear of dark wall colours (which isn't too difficult when you rent: chances are your wall colours will already be neutral anyway).

2. GENERAL LIGHTING

General lighting is intended to light up a room in its entirety. In other words, it is the main light source that will do most of the illuminating within a space. Examples of this type of lighting can include spot lights or down lights, chandeliers and ceiling pendants.

3. TASK LIGHTING

Task lighting sheds light on the specific tasks a person carries out in a given space, such as reading, cooking, writing and so on. Examples can include floor lamps, wall-mounted lights and desk lamps.

4. ACCENT LIGHTING

Accent lighting adds visual interest to architectural features, art or plants. It can also be used to create a focal point when placed under cabinets or on bookcases.

WHAT CAN YOU DO?

Now, unless your landlord is happy for you to hire an electrician (and most aren't, in my experience), there's not much you can do when it comes to lighting, apart from change a pendant shade. Even if you were to install new light fixtures, there is no guarantee you would be able to take them with you to your next home, so it's a wasted investment.

Instead, focus your effort on the other types of lighting that don't require the same commitment, in particular, plug-in lights. They are affordable, and immediately elevate the look of a temporary or short-term space.

HOW TO DEAL WITH POOR LIGHTING

Here are some inexpensive ways to improve on poor lighting, and most of these are plug-in lights.

LED LIGHT BULBS

Before anything else, you need to switch your bulbs to LED ones. They last longer and consume less energy, so you save money in the long run.

CHANGE YOUR LAMPSHADES

Apart from potentially being on the unattractive side, maybe your existing lampshade looks very dark and doesn't seem to be letting out much light? Opt for lighter shades that will allow more illumination. You can often find inexpensive shades at charity shops or thrift stores.

UNDER-CABINET LIGHTING

This will give you all the light you need when working on your kitchen counters. You can buy LED light tracks or battery-operated lights that can be stuck to the underside of cabinets and easily removed when you leave.

PLUG-IN WALL-MOUNTED LIGHTS (SCONCES)

These lights attach directly to the wall to provide task or accent lighting – perfect when there isn't enough floor space. They can be plugged into wall plugs and hung from brackets or hooks. If they aren't too heavy, self-adhesive hooks can be used to hold them in place.

OVERHEAD PENDANT LIGHT

It's no suprise that rental properties often don't have good overhead lighting. But the good news is you can add your own ceiling pendant lights without needing an electrician. By using cup hooks in the ceiling, you can suspend plug-in pendants from covered cords or chains. Alternatively, you can buy a plug-in cord with a bulb and add a classic lampshade, if that is more to your style. But it is worth noting that pendants hung in this way work best in homes with high ceilings.

Good lighting is so important, and there is absolutely no reason why you should live without it, in darkness.

FLOOR LAMPS/TABLE LAMPS

These lights can be placed in the corners of a room or on surfaces to amplify the amount of light in a room. Table lamps can be placed on hall tables, sideboards, bedside tables, or desks. Depending on the style (upward or downward lighting), floor lamps can be positioned to shine light over sofas, chairs or side units.

BATTERY-OPERATED LED LIGHTS

Strategically place these stick-on lights in closets, wardrobes, pantries or other tight spots to brighten up the space.

CANDLES

These offer a cosy glow. For maximum effect, place them next to mirrors, windows or in glass or metallic containers. I love placing tealights inside glass mason jars.

UPDATING LIGHT SWITCHES

DO. NOT. PAINT. THEM. I repeat, do not paint light switches. It looks tacky (in my opinion) and I know landlords aren't usually fans of this. But you can successfully cover them – with washi tape or contact paper.

Before applying contact paper, turn off your electricity, unscrew the light-switch plate from the wall. Stick the contact paper to it. Cut a small slit at each corner, fold all the sides down and trim any excess paper. Finally, cut an opening for the light switch and screws with a craft knife.

WINDOWS

Window dressings aren't just for decoration purposes. There are actually many different ways in which your home benefits from them – hence, they are worth spending time and money getting right. (And yes, that applies to rented homes, too.)

Window treatments:

- Allow you to control the amount of daylight in your home
- Provide privacy
- Help to insulate a house by blocking out any external heat or cold

While it is a landlord's duty to ensure that the windows in their property are in good condition, they aren't under any obligation to provide window dressings for tenants – even if the property is a furnished one.

However, that isn't to say that every property will come without curtains or blinds – I've found quite the opposite. Most of the properties I've lived in have had a window dressing of some sort. Whether those curtains or blinds were to my taste, or even clean was a different matter altogether.

I would always advise changing window dressings when renting, just because it's often really easy to do. This could include adding decorative curtains to a window that already has blinds in place or swapping vertical blinds for something a little less average, such as split bamboo or Roman blinds. Try your very best to work with what you already have. By this, I mean reuse any tracks or holes that are already there, to avoid the hassle of having to create fresh new holes that will need to be filled in. And remember, if you are removing any window dressing entirely, always store it in a safe space so it can be put back once you leave.

CURTAINS

What can you do if your home doesn't already have holes for curtain poles or track and the landlord is completely against you putting up your own?

Well, you can try explaining that you would be more than happy to fill in the holes before you leave, or keep the fixings in place for the next tenant – who you're sure will find them quite helpful.

Still a no?

Don't worry, as thankfully there are other renter-friendly options for hanging fabric panels or curtains.

SELF-ADHESIVE HOOKS

I've already said how revolutionary these self-adhesive products are, and I wasn't kidding. They can be used to attach more than pictures to the wall. Secure two adhesive hooks (and another in the centre if your windows are quite large) to the wall above your window, and balance a lightweight curtain rod on the hooks. You can even add a little touch of glamour by painting the hooks and rail in a brass or matt black paint.

But please note, this may not be the best option if you have young kids who might pull at these curtains, as they need to be handled with care.

TENSION RODS

This will only work if your window is recessed. The tension rod can be extended to push against the sides of the recess and can be dressed with lightweight curtains. They can be placed at different heights at a window, depending on your style.

STRIPS OF VELCRO

Velcro strips can be stitched to one side of a curtain panel and then the corresponding strips attached directly to the wall. This works for hanging up net curtains on UPVC window frames or for windows that don't need the curtains to be opened and closed often (on a glass-panel door, perhaps?).

 I would always advise changing window dressings when renting, just because it's often really easy to do.

CURTAINS FROM THE CEILING

Do you think your landlord would be more likely to say yes to a few screw holes in the ceiling rather than the wall? It's worth a try. There are wire suspension curtain rails that can be attached to the ceiling, and are great for adding height and elegance to a window.

And before I move on to my next topic, here are some dos and don'ts of curtain hanging:

DO

- Ensure your curtain rails are wider than your window. This tricks the eye into thinking the window is bigger than it is and ensures the window frames are always covered (even with open curtains).

- Measure your window's width to ensure you are using enough fabric. You want to use enough fabric to create a beautiful gathered effect. Anything less can look a little limp.

- Change your curtains with the seasons. You might want light linen or cotton curtains for warmer weather and fully lined velvet drapes for the colder months.

DON'T

- Hang your curtains too low. The higher the curtain rails, the taller your window will seem. So keep your rails as close to the ceiling as possible.

- Don't go too short. The curtain should fall to the floor or at least to 2–3cm (around 1in) above the floor. Unless, of course, you are using cafe-style curtains.

OTHER WINDOW TREATMENTS

Of course, curtains are not the only way to dress a window. If you want to go for a different approach, there are plenty of other options. Blinds or film will take up less space and can often create a much more contemporary look.

FAUX WOOD VENETIAN BLINDS

These blinds will almost certainly look better than any current aluminium or plastic Venetian blinds your window might have, so swap them for these. Because they aren't real they are much more affordable, too. And there are lots of different finishes and colours to match your décor.

SELF-ADHESIVE WINDOW FILM

Window film is, as the name suggests, removable plastic film that is applied to your windows. It sticks either because it has an adhesive backing, or by static cling. There are many different types of film, and they have several functions. Some have helpful properties such as blocking incoming heat from the sun, some are designed to cut down on glare, but most are simply for privacy reasons. Window film works really well on sliding doors or on windows in a bathroom where other treatments might not be as effective.

BRING THE OUTDOORS IN

Plants and flowers inject an instant hit of life and character into a space (see pages 160–7 for my plant guide), so why not place some by your window? Bright, fresh flowers will draw attention away from damaged or old window frames, and many plants will thrive in the sunlight. You could even create your own herb garden by the window in your kitchen. Not only will it look great, but your cooking will benefit, too.

And if you are able to put a window box outside your window, even better – you will be able to enjoy it every time you see it from both outside and inside your home.

BEDSHEETS AS CURTAINS

This is great alternative to actual curtains, if you can't find any the correct length or just can't afford them. Depending on your window size, you can purchase two single (twin) flat sheets or one king-size sheet and cut it in half down the middle and hem the raw edges. You can hang it on curtain rails by creating a channel at the top for the rail to fit through (see step 5 of the no-sew cabinet curtain skirt project on page 183), or by using clip-on curtain hooks. Patterned bedsheets work well in kids' rooms, and plain colours can always be decorated with fabric paint.

BAMBOO BLINDS

These are great and can be applied to the inner or outer frame of a window. There are many styles and colours to choose from so you'll be spoilt for choice. Opt for tones that don't clash but that complement and contrast with your flooring and walls.

Just one thing to note: most bamboo blinds require the installation of brackets. However, there are a few that come with the type of brackets used for hanging pictures, which only need a small cup hook or nail to secure them in position.

CUSTOMIZED VINYL OR FABRIC ROLLER BLINDS

These are usually fitted to the insides of the window recess (and require holes to be drilled). You can have them custom-made, or buy ones that can be cut to size at home. Ensure you are meticulous with your measurements and allow space for the spring mechanism and brackets in your measurements. Sometimes the property may already have these types of blinds installed – so use the existing brackets to hang your own.

You can also cover the front of any bland or boring blind with a fabric of your choice – as long as it isn't too thick or textured – using fabric spray adhesive.

A no-screw option is compression roller blinds that fit snugly into a window recess without having to drill holes. They are a little more expensive but a great investment if you plan to rent long-term.

SOME OTHER POINTERS FOR RENTERS

BUY IRON-ON HEMMING TAPE

In case you're not a dab hand with the sewing machine, this is a great tool for making adjustments to the lengths of curtains – whether new ones or those you might have brought with you from your previous home.

BUY CLIP-ON CURTAIN HOOKS

These are super-handy if you've just moved into a property that has a curtain rail but no curtains (and you don't own any). Clip on a large piece of fabric or a plain bedsheet (see opposite) until you've got the time and money to go out and buy yourself curtains.

INVEST IN ADJUSTABLE CURTAIN RAILS

If you are allowed to put up curtain rails, invest in the type that expand to different sizes. That way, you can reuse them for other windows in the future.

You can also use unusual materials for rails, such as steel or copper pipes. And if you are looking for even more budget-friendly ideas for curtain rails, try using a painted PVC pipe or wooden dowelling.

CREATE YOUR OWN DESIGNER CURTAINS

Designer curtains often work out to be expensive, so why not jazz up your existing curtains with a little fabric paint, dye or iron-on decals?

Why not jazz up your existing curtains with a little fabric paint, dye or decals?

HOME ACCESSORIES

I remember that moment I decided to order a yellow velvet sofa. I remember the excitement, the feeling that I was rebelling against some great, unspoken sofa-buying rule that dictated you should choose neutral colours such as grey, cream or navy.

I also remember the look of horror on my husband's face when I told him what I had done.

'You did what now?'

I repeated myself.

'But velvet…and yellow…' his voice sounded pained.

'It'll be fine,' I reassured him.

And it was fine. More than fine, actually.

The sofa, when it arrived, immediately changed the feel of our living room from drab to fab.

The walls no longer seemed as plain. The blinds that hung at the window behind the sofa no longer looked as mediocre. The laminate flooring contrasted better with the sofa than with anything else. Every inch of décor in my living room felt rejuvenated.

Heck, I was rejuvenated just looking at it.

And the best part?

A week after the sofa was delivered, my husband said, 'I'm so glad you chose this sofa.'

Can I get an eye roll please?

Because there are quite a lot of things that you can't change when renting, it's really important that you focus on the things that *can* be changed. In most cases, that would include items such as home accessories and soft furnishings.

Spend your money on pieces that will add character and colour to a room, and that can easily be taken with you when you move on to your next home. In this chapter, I'll cover all the small things – those little touches that will help to personalize your rented home. The stuff that most renters tend to forget about but that, actually, makes the biggest impact. And there are a few DIY projects too, just in case you fancy having a go at making a few of your own custom furniture pieces.

FURNISHED OR UNFURNISHED?

Rented properties come fully furnished, part-furnished or unfurnished.

FULLY FURNISHED

Fully furnished properties include all the essential white goods, as well as other furniture such as tables, beds, chairs and so on. Basically, everything needed for you to move in straight away.

PART-FURNISHED

Part furnished properties include some of the basic items you will need, but also allow you to move in some of your own furniture.

UNFURNISHED

You'll get the bare bones in an unfurnished property, but it will include things such as light fittings and flooring.

PROS AND CONS

Personally, I much prefer to rent an unfurnished home because it allows for additional flexibility when it comes to decorating. And, as the furniture is mine, there isn't the worry that I might be held liable by the landlord for any sort of damage that might occur.

On the flipside, though, there are lots of people who prefer the idea of renting a property that is fully furnished, as it takes away the worry of having to pay for start-up pieces of furniture, which can become costly. And if you're the type that moves around a lot, having everything already there and accessible is super-convenient.

But whether your home is furnished or unfurnished, home accessories are definitely the most effective way of bringing personality and style to a space.

THE HOW-TO GUIDE

Now, I'm not about to dictate the sort of home furnishings you should have in your house because, like most things in the interiors world, styles will vary and there really is no one-size-fits-all set of rules. However, if this were a general renter's guide to furnishing a home, it would probably read something like this.

INVEST IN STATEMENT PIECES

Furniture might just be the only way that you will be able to add personality to your rented home, so think of it as an investment worth focusing your energy on. In the same way that I chose a luxurious mustard-yellow velvet sofa for my living room, try to do similar. Introduce at least one statement item per room that will play the main character.

- Choose bold colours that will stand out well against neutral walls.
- Opt for furniture that has beautiful textures and attractive details.
- Break up furniture sets. Mix and match the materials and styles of your furniture. For example, there's no reason why you can't have a rustic wooden farmhouse table paired with heavy-duty industrial chairs. Variety just creates more interest, which in turn makes for an overall compelling look.

Statement pieces also draw attention away from the more permanent features you'd rather people didn't notice – the wall with the cracked air vent, for example?

You get the picture: either go big or go home. And big doesn't have to mean expensive, which brings me to my next two points.

BUY SECOND HAND

If you are looking to buy any additional items for your home, start off by sourcing furniture from local charity stores or online second-hand sites. Not only is it more eco-friendly, but it can also save you lots of money. One man's trash is another man's treasure, and all that.

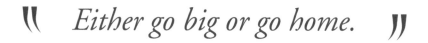

Either go big or go home.

BE UNCOVENTIONAL

Be creative with how you use your furniture, and with the pieces you choose to use as furniture. For example:

- Use unusual pieces such as a tree stump, wooden pallet or vintage suitcase as a coffee table or side table.

- Stools, crates or stacked magazines can all be used as bedroom nightstands.

- A tall, narrow bookcase can be laid on its side to become a bench with seating and storage.

- Copper pipes can be used to make plant stands or shelving.

CUSTOMIZE AND UPCYCLE

If you are renting a furnished home, then opt for making small, damage-free improvements to any furniture provided. Replacing the handles on cupboards and wardrobes, or using removable wallpaper are all good ways to change the look of what's there already.

If you are looking to update your own furniture, you'll have much more freedom with how you choose to change it.

CHOOSE OPEN-STYLE STORAGE

I touched on this in the previous chapter: the open nature of furniture such as bookcases, crates and any other large storage units gives you more wiggle room for personalization. Fill your shelves with your favourite books, trinkets, materials and mementos from trips (but don't go overboard, its easy to get carried away and create a cluttered look).

If that furniture happens to roll, too, even better. Mobile furniture offers a lot of versatility for short-term rentals. You'll be able to use the same table or cart around your home for multiple purposes.

Why not buy a second hand rolling bar cart and give it a little update? You can use it as a way to display some of your luxurious items.

ADD SOFT FURNISHINGS WHEN YOU CAN

Your rented property may have come furnished, which can mean you're equipped with large pieces of furniture that you don't love and can't replace. Thankfully, it's easy to tailor these pieces to your style by decorating them with soft furnishings you love. None of the items below need cost the earth.

- Adding cushions and throws can be a really easy way to add colour to a room. Buy cushions in bold fabrics or classic designs, and mix them up. They are also pretty practical since throws and cushion covers can be laundered – unlike a sofa.

- Area rugs do a great job of disguising any unattractive marks on the floor, but items such as large floor cushions, faux fur throws and bean bags do just as well.

- Buy covers for your sofa. For example, consider covering a cold, tired leather sofa with a stylish sofa cover. These come in many different shapes, colours, fabrics and patterns – and some can even be custom-made to fit the exact size of your sofa. Size is important, you really don't want your sofa standing out for all the wrong reasons.

- Tablecloths are perfect for hiding marks or stains on a dining table, or disguising a colour that isn't to your liking.

- For your own furniture, you could reupholster chairs or stools in fun, playful fabrics of your choosing. You can also buy seat pads or removable covers to go over tired seats.

PROJECT #12

DIY RE-COVER A STOOL OR CHAIR

If you have worn-out chair seats, you can easily re-cover them. In this tutorial I'll share how to re-cover, update and greatly an improve a chair or stool.

SUPPLIES

- Bar stool or chair with drop-in or screw-on seat
- Protective gloves
- Screwdriver
- Flat-head screwdriver
- Pliers
- Upholstery foam (optional)
- Fabric, large enough to cover stool seat with additional 15cm (6in) around each edge
- Pencil
- Ruler
- Scissors
- Heavy-duty staple gun

A few things to note:

- A word of warning – this project will not work for all types of furniture. Certain items of furniture, such as chairs with sprung seats and antique pieces, will need to be upholstered professionally.
- But if you have picked up some old stools from the flea market, or have discovered some shabby chairs in your parents' attic, this is an easy way to update them. It will work for any items with drop-in or screw-on seats, and is achievable for anyone with some pliers, fabric and a heavy-duty staple gun.

Put your gloves on, especially if your stool or chair is looking a little grimy. In fact, at this point, it might be a good idea to give your stool or chair a thorough clean.

Remove the screws from the underside of the seat to detach it from the stool. Keep the screws in a safe place.

Take off the existing fabric by removing the staples. A flat-head screwdriver and pliers might help here. If the upholstery foam is in good condition, you won't need to replace it. But if it is damaged, remove it and use it as a template to cut a new foam pad to the same size.

Place the fabric right-side down. Position the stool seat centrally on top, and rotate it to suit the grain or pattern of the fabric. Draw around the outline with a pencil. Put the seat to one side.

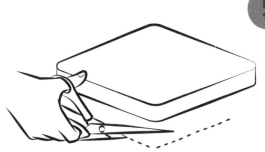

Draw a second outline, 15cm (6in) outside the first, to give a wide border that will be wrapped around the edges of the stool seat. Cut along this line with your scissors.

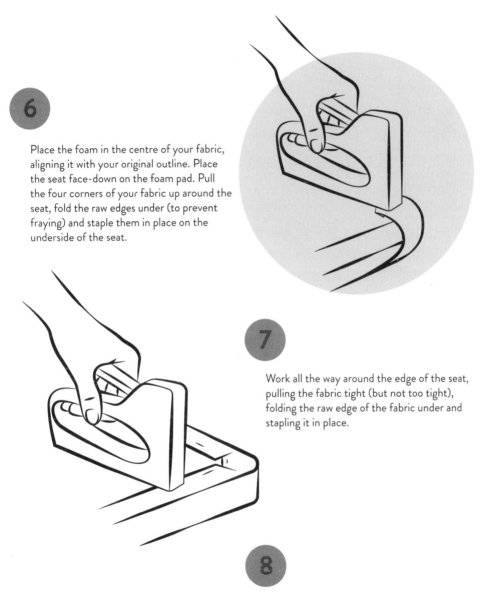

6

Place the foam in the centre of your fabric, aligning it with your original outline. Place the seat face-down on the foam pad. Pull the four corners of your fabric up around the seat, fold the raw edges under (to prevent fraying) and staple them in place on the underside of the seat.

7

Work all the way around the edge of the seat, pulling the fabric tight (but not too tight), folding the raw edge of the fabric under and stapling it in place.

8

Reattach the cushion to the stool.

PROJECT #13

HOW TO PAINT FURNITURE

How do you transform a battered old cupboard – or even something flat-pack and basic – into something modern and lovable? Painting old wooden furniture will always be a controversial topic, especially when you are painting what others might deem to be something antique or valuable.

My thoughts on this whole matter: you do you. It's your house, your style, your item. If painting something will make you feel happier, then that is the only rationale that counts for anything.

SUPPLIES
- Household cleaner
- Wood filler and putty knife (optional)
- Sandpaper (medium grit)
- Cloth
- Primer
- Paint of your choice (emulsion, chalk paint, gloss)
- Smooth paint roller
- Paintbrush
- Clear (polyurethane) varnish or colourless wax

A few things to note:
- There are a million different furniture-painting tutorials online, and sometimes it can feel a little overwhelming trying to decide which of them will work for you. Over the years, I have tried many methods and the one I'm about to share is hands down the best way to go about it. It's certainly not the quickest – but it gives you professional-looking results. So I hope you find this guide useful, should you ever find a gem being chucked out that is crying out for a facelift.
- There are lots of different types of primer, suitable for lots of different materials. If you are painting a laminate surface, I would recommend using an oil-based primer.

1 If your furniture has drawers, hardware or doors, remove them and work on them individually.

2 I can't stress enough how important it is to clean the furniture. It will prevent paint from cracking or peeling off in the future. Give the item a very good clean with household cleaner.

3 Fill any holes or missing veneer with a putty knife and wood filler. Apply the wood filler to any damaged areas and smooth it with the putty knife. Leave to dry.

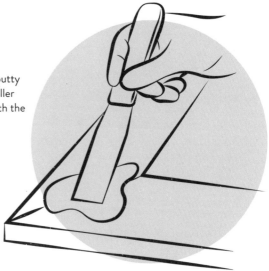

4 Now you need to sand your furniture. Sanding will help remove any existing paint, gloss or varnish, and will give your primer something to adhere to. Use medium-grit sandpaper. Wipe away any loose dust with a cloth. If at this stage you find there are any further cracks or holes, use wood filler to fill them, as in step 3, and wait for it to dry. Then rub the filled area with sandpaper.

5

Apply the primer with a smooth paint roller or good-quality paintbrush. Primer will help the paint adhere to the furniture and will also cover any stains or wood discoloration. This step is important, especially if you are painting laminate, melamine or a varnished piece. Once the primer is dry, sand again lightly for an even finish.

6

Apply a coat of paint using a roller (a brush may leave brushstroke marks) for the main surfaces, and a brush to for the hard-to-reach crevices and corners.

7

Once the paint is dry (follow the manufacturer's instructions for drying times), seal your furniture. Sealing provides extra protection for the paint finish and also creates a wipeable, easy-to-clean surface. You have two options: paint with clear polyurethane varnish that is non-yellowing, using the same method as for the top coat, or rub on some colourless wax (although this is not as hard-wearing as varnish). To apply wax, wipe it on with a cloth, leave it for 10–15 minutes and then buff it with a clean, soft cloth for a shiny finish. Leave it to cure for at least a day.

8

Now put all the hardware back on, and you are done.

PROJECT #14

DIY BENCH

Want some extra seating but don't want to splash out on new chairs? Then make your own! This DIY bench looks great, and is really versatile. Try placing it alongside your dining table, or style it with cushions and baskets and use it to fill the bare space in your hallway.

This project probably looks far harder than it is. But don't be daunted by the prospect of creating your own piece of furniture – it's just connecting some wood to hairpin legs, and that's pretty much it. Simple.

SUPPLIES

- 3 hardwood timber planks of equal sizes, each at least 4cm (1½in) thick
- Sanding machine
- 2 heavy strap ties
- 3.8cm (1½in) screws
- Wood stain or paint of your choice
- Paint-stirring stick
- Paintbrush
- Clear varnish (polyurethane), if using paint instead of wood stain
- Tape measure
- 4 hairpin legs, 40cm (16 in) long, with screws

A few things to note:
- You will need three wooden planks for this project, of equal sizes. For my bench, I used planks that were 100cm (40in) long. You can often get wood cut to size at larger DIY stores, or you can buy standard lengths and cut it yourself.
- When sourcing your wood, the thicker the better – you need it to be at least 4cm (1½in) thick. You want your bench to be be sturdy and strong.

1

Sand each plank with a sanding machine.
Pay particular attention to the sides
and edges.

2

Position the three wooden planks next to
each other, so that they line up perfectly.
Connect the three planks together using
two heavy strap ties – one at either end
of the bench seat for support. Use
3.8cm (1½in) screws to secure the
heavy strap ties in place.

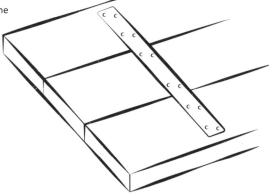

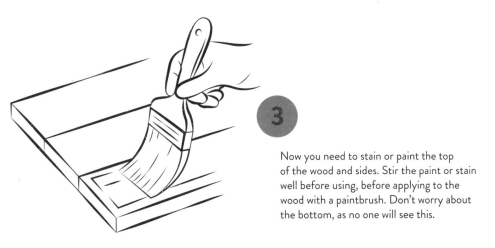

Now you need to stain or paint the top of the wood and sides. Stir the paint or stain well before using, before applying to the wood with a paintbrush. Don't worry about the bottom, as no one will see this.

4

If you have painted the wood (instead of using wood stain), you now need to seal the wood with varnish. Open a can of clear varnish (polyurethane), stir well and then use a paintbrush to apply to the bench.

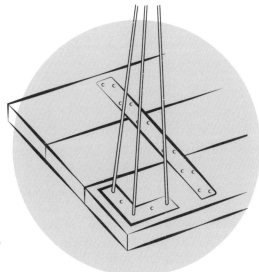

Use your tape measure to mark in each corner where each hairpin leg will need to be attached. Attach the hairpin legs to each corner of the bench, according to the manufacturer's guidelines.

HOW TO DRESS A BED

In the same way that soft furnishing such as cushions and throws can make a huge difference to a sofa, bed linen can have a similar impact on a bed. Even if a bedframe looks a little tired and the bedroom seems bland and neutral, the addition of some pattern and colour can elevate bed into a focal point. And the best part? Bed linen is easy to change, month to month or year to year, giving your room a different look each time.

PICK A THEME AND COLOUR

This will help to narrow down your colour palette and, ultimately, the bed linen, cushions and accessories you select as a result. Look for the colours repeated in your bedroom through pictures or other décor and try to reflect that in your bedding.

If you want a minimal, classic look, stick to pale neutrals and crisp whites, but mix rich textures and abstract prints so the bed doesn't end up looking too plain.

If you want bright and bold, this can usually be achieved by introducing colourful throws or decorative cushions and keeping the sheets plain white. Or you could, of course, buy coloured or patterned duvet sets.

CHOOSE HIGH-QUALITY BEDDING

Now is not the time to scrimp on cash. Investing in high-quality bedding will give your bed a luxurious finish. The most common choice for bedding is cotton, but linen is another good option. It is slightly more expensive but very durable, so it can work out cheaper in the long-run.

Here are just a few things you might need to dress a bed (ensure you get the sizing right).

- **Mattress cover:** if your mattress is already provided but not new, invest in a comfortable mattress topper, both for hygiene reasons and added comfort.

- **Fitted sheets:** opt for an extra-deep version if you are using a mattress topper.

- **Valance sheet:** this decorative sheet is designed to conceal the base of a bed. Some might find it a little outdated but it's great for concealing an ugly bedframe.

- **Duvet and duvet covers:** Choose duvet covers that complement the colours in the room.

- **Pillows (rectangular) and pillow cases:** you can buy pillowcases with or without the traditional flap that the end of the pillow tucks into.

- **Feature (accent) cushions:** play around with sizes and colour.

- **Throw:** folded at the end of the bed, a throw can add warmth, colour or pattern and texture – try velvet, faux-fur or wool.

And the best part? Bed linen is easy to change, month to month or year to year, giving your room a different look each time.

ADD DECORATIVE CUSHIONS

Now it's time to choose your cushions. The styles you opt for will depend on your bedding and colour scheme. The key is to mix it up to achieve depth and contrast. Combine shapes (square or rectangular), prints (stripes, abstract, chevron) and textures (quilted, velvet, linen, sequins).

DRESS THE END OF THE BED

Add a throw, chunky-knit blanket, faux fur or folded quilt to the end of the bed, either at an angle or in layers. For warmer climates, opt for lighter fabrics and knits.

RENTER-FRIENDLY HEADBOARDS

Headboards are the perfect solution if the wall behind your bed is looking bland.

- Apply removable wallpaper to the bottom half of the wall behind your bed.
- Hang a tapestry or light rug the width of the bed with adhesive hooks or strips.
- Prop up shutters or old doors against the wall behind the bed.
- Draw a fun geometric outline or skyline with washi tape.
- Add bookcases behind the bed to increase storage and display options.
- Attach a plain sheet of plywood to the wall behind the bed and customize it with paint or decals.
- Add super-large pillows and cushions.

MORE IDEAS

You can use tablecloths or any piece of fabric to dress the end of the bed.

Use pallets as a base for your bed, if you can't afford to buy a bedframe or divan. Make sure the pallets are sanded and treated before placing your mattress on top.

ROOM DIVIDERS

So we know that knocking down walls or adding in new partition walls
to a rented home is out of the question. But if you're living in a space that
has no clearly defined zones (a studio apartment perhaps), or maybe you just
want to create a little privacy, what's a girl (or guy) to do? A room divider
might be just what you need.

There are many different styles of room divider – and many ways to create a division that is temporary, stylish and effective. Here are some ideas:

USING FURNITURE

You can divide up a space using furniture. This could include a large, open storage unit (such as an open bookcase on wheels) or a large cupboard. Or you could use stacked crates secured safely together.

CURTAINS

Hang sheer nets or curtains from a tension pole (if you don't want to create holes) or curtain rail. You can also drape curtains over clothing rails.

GARDEN TRELLIS PANELS

You could create a screen by tying a few garden trellis panels together with string.

BUY A TRADITIONAL FOLDING SCREEN

Should I have started with this option?

PLANTS

I've owned my fair share of plants over the years (sadly a lot never made it past the second week), which is why I can write the next few sentences with such conviction.

Indoor plants are probably the best way to add character to a rented home. In fact, if my editor had told me I could only choose one section for this book, this would be the one.

A huge statement to make, but here's why:

- Houseplants are affordable.
- They bring the outside in and, frankly, you can never go wrong with a little greenery in your life.
- Plants are great air cleansers.
- You can't have too many. Fact.

Of course, plants need to be well looked after in order to grow and thrive. And if you think that watering them and occasionally feeding them is all that's required, I have heard that to really care for them properly, you should talk to them, too. Even name them, sing to them… Easy enough if you have the time to pander to such demands. However, if you don't have the gift of 'green fingers' or a 'green thumb', like myself, this is where you're going to struggle.

So, here, I am going to show you the best ways to introduce plants to your home.

PLACING PLANTS

Remember that plants like daylight, and some need more than others. Read the label to see just how tolerant a plant is to sun or shade and place it in your home with this in mind.

BUY INDOOR PLANTS THAT REQUIRE MINIMAL CARE

Basically, if you forget to water them one day, or forget their name, they won't hold a grudge and decide to die on you (a total 'cut off your nose to spite your face' situation). In my 'expert' opinion, here are some of the best indoor plants.

Of course, there are almost unlimited varieties of cacti and succulents out there, so do some research and choose the ones you like best. And remember to check how large they will grow, before committing to buying them.

WHERE TO PUT THEM?

Place some of the plants on your coffee table and bedside table. Group plants at different heights for greater impact. Larger indoor plants, such as the beautiful fiddle-leaf fig tree *(Ficus lyrata)*, can be placed in lovely pots in bare corners or to mask ugly fixtures. Place plants on windowsills, especially the ones that need plenty of sunlight. Or suspend hanging plants from ropes or chains to add beauty to the heights of your room.

Cactus

Succulent

Mother-in-law's tongue
(Sansevieria trifasciata)

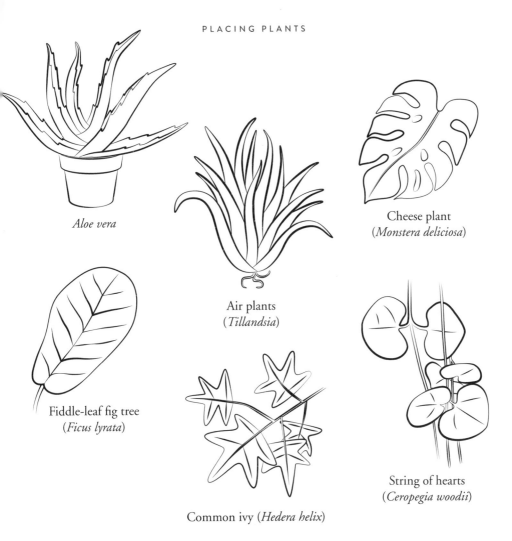

Aloe vera

Air plants
(*Tillandsia*)

Cheese plant
(*Monstera deliciosa*)

Fiddle-leaf fig tree
(*Ficus lyrata*)

Common ivy (*Hedera helix*)

String of hearts
(*Ceropegia woodii*)

STILL NOT CONVINCED?

Why not try faux plants? Hear me out. There are actually some amazing faux plants you can buy. As in, you'd really have to look quite closely to prove they weren't real. Faux plants have the advantage of not needing any daylight, so they are a perfect choice for dark corners or rooms with no natural light, such as some bathrooms.

PROJECT #15

TEN-MINUTE PLANT-POT BAGS

Plants can be placed in a variety of aesthetically pleasing pots – baskets, crates, ceramic pots, you name it. My favourite, though, are plant bags. They are easy and cheap to make – and you can play around with a variety of sizes and designs to suit your plants (and home).

SUPPLIES

- Brown packing paper/ Kraft paper
- Sticky-back vinyl paper (matt), the same size as the brown paper
- Scissors
- Super glue
- Tape

A few things to note:

- Just to be clear, these bags should be used for plants in plastic pots – don't put your plants directly into the bags with bare earth, as you won't be able to water them effectively. Make sure your plants are in standard plastic pots with drainage holes. That way, you can remove them from the bags when you need to water them. The bags are waterproof and you can wipe the insides clean whenever you want to.
- You will need brown packing paper or Kraft paper for this project, but why not use a paper with a pattern? The plant pots work really effectively when made with polka dot brown paper, as shown in the photograph.
- For these bags, I cut my paper from a 50cm x 10m (20in x 11yd) roll, but you will need to measure your paper against your plant pot and cut accordingly – see instructions overleaf.
- Once you've got the hang of the method, why not try decorating the outside of your plant pots? You could paint colourful patterns or add letters and shapes with stencils to give them a really personal touch.

1

First, you will need to cut the packing paper and sticky-back vinyl paper to your desired width and height. Use your plant pot as a guide, and make sure your paper is at least 2.5cm (1in) longer than the pot's height.

2

Next, apply the sticky-back vinyl paper to one side of the packing paper, as a single, complete piece. If you notice any areas on the packing paper that aren't covered with sticky vinyl, cut some more off and fill in gaps, overlapping the edges. It doesn't matter if this part isn't neat because no one will see it!

3

Flip your paper over so the brown side is facing up and cut off any excess contact paper edges with your scissors. You should be left with a much more durable paper that is brown on one side and vinyl paper on the other.

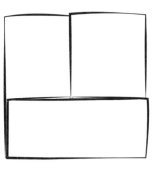

5

Take the plastic pot your plant is sitting in and measure its diameter. Fold the bottom of your paper upwards by that measurement, plus an extra few centimetres/inches. This will become the base of your plant bag so it's important that it's the right size – the longer the fold-up, the wider the base.

Place the rectangle of paper horizontally (landscape) in front of you with the vinyl side facing up. Straighten the paper and fold over the left and right edges so that the ends meet in the middle (with a small overlap). Remember, the side covered with vinyl paper will become the inside of your bag, so make sure that only the brown side is visible at this point. Glue the two overlapping edges together. You should end up with a rectangular shape.

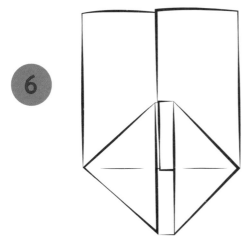

6 Make a diamond shape with the folded base and press it flat, as shown. Do this by opening out the fold-up and folding both corners into the centre.

7 Fold the top and bottom edges of the diamond shape into the centre. Secure in place with glue and then tape – for added strength.

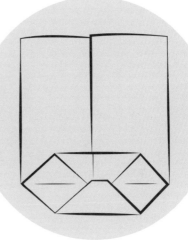

8 Open up the top of the planter bag and place your hands inside to shape it into a cylinder with a firm base. Roll the top edge over so the inner sticky-back vinyl paper shows. Keep rolling until you are happy with the height. Scrunch the bag to give it that added texture.

BUILT-INS

My husband and I have very different opinions on what makes a house rentable. Being the sensible sort, he looks at the affordability, location, heating and so on. I, on the other hand, will be swayed by the design features, the door handles, the height of the ceilings…

But, to present a united front during a house viewing, we pretend. We pretend that our differing opinions don't exist, smiling in sync and nodding in agreement.

Until that moment. This moment.

Letting agent: 'So what do you think?'

My husband: 'Can you give us a moment?'

He turns to me and the act is dropped.

He starts: 'I really like this house. Did you notice how warm it feels? It must have really good insulation.'

Me: 'The cupboards in the kitchen! Did you see them? I thought they looked ugly. And grungy.'

Him: 'I love the size of the garden, too. Maybe we'll be able to have a proper family barbecue.'

Me: 'Yes, but those kitchen cupboards…'

Him: 'And there's the garage. You'll finally have a place to store all of your junk– um, unfinished projects.'

Me: 'Erm, are you hearing me? The kitchen!'

Him: 'Minor details, Medina.'

Me: 'Not really. I'll have to cook in it!'

Him: 'But you don't cook…'

By built-ins, I mean the fixtures in your home
that you aren't allowed to change. For example,
the laminate countertop in the kitchen (that
is rotting from water damage), or perhaps the
custom-built fitted wardrobe in the bedroom
(with the very eccentric-looking sliding doors).

These kinds of features are ones that would
require some degree of renovation if they were
ever to be removed or replaced. And the word
'renovation', well, you won't find it in any renter's
guidebook I'd be likely to recommend. But
perhaps you'll see it mentioned in one of those
'five sure-fire ways to get yourself kicked out
of a rental' type of articles.

So that's the long and the short of what this
chapter is all about. Good chat on ways to make
all those practical features a little more attractive.

THE JOY OF BUILT-INS

Sometimes landlords do a really good job of getting built-in features right. 'Right', here, refers to designs that support a renter's living needs well, while also looking aesthetically pleasing to the eye. And sometimes they really do not.

Reasons for the latter can include practicality, dependability or affordability. No doubt there are more – basically all the '–itys' that don't fill you with excitement.

To be perfectly honest, there will be a few things in this chapter that won't evoke any Marie Kondo-esque 'spark joy' reaction. And others that will make you frown and think, 'God Medina, is this stuff really necessary?' Which I get. I can hardly expect you to get excited about changing a toilet seat, now can I? (Unless, of course, those sorts of things rock your world – to which I can't comment).

But, to answer that earlier question, yes. Yes, it is necessary.

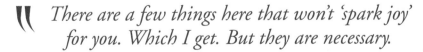

There are a few things here that won't 'spark joy' for you. Which I get. But they are necessary.

THE CUPBOARDS

Whether in the kitchen, bedroom or bathroom, there are lots of options when it comes to updating or improving your cupboards.

REMOVE THE DOORS

This will create openness, a better flow, and give your room a more modern look.

It can be done in less than an hour. All you need to do is grab a screwdriver (or an electric screwdriver, if you want to speed up the process further) and unscrew all of the cupboard door hinges from the cabinet frames.

You will need to put the doors back on before you leave the property – which, again, won't take much time – so make sure the doors you remove are stored away in a safe and dry place (usually the garage or the attic). Put each set of screws into a bag and tape it to the corresponding door so there is less chance of you misplacing them.

Once the doors are removed, you have three options:

1. **Leave the cabinets open**
   If nothing else, this will teach you to be a little neater, as your dishes, clothes and so on will now be on display. If you are doing this in the kitchen, I would recommend only removing the doors from the top cabinets. That way, you can still store food cans and packets (not the best things to look at) in the lower units.

2. **Attach your own choice of doors**
   You can usually get doors built to the exact dimensions of your existing frames, especially in the kitchen. This is a costly option, but something to consider if you are renting a long-term property and are a little more invested in its upkeep.

3. **Hang curtains (in other words, skirted cabinets)**
   Yes, skirted cabinets can be used in homes that aren't your traditional 'country' style. They're great for modern homes too, provided you choose a fabric that is fun and… modern. Ha! Curtains under the counters can be an interesting way to introduce pattern and colour into a boring space. They can be attached using a tension rod, or with adhesive hooks and dowels. I'll be sharing how to make your own a little later on (see page 180).

REPLACE THE HARDWARE

It's simple, but it can make the world of difference. Replacing the hardware can transform the most ordinary of built-in cupboards/drawers into something quite luxe and high-end looking. Find cupboard handles or knobs that are more to your taste and switch them over. To avoid drilling new holes, make sure your chosen hardware matches up with the existing holes in the cupboard. Store the old pulls/handles in a safe place.

COVER/LINE THE SHELVES

Maybe the cupboard frames are in good condition but the shelves themselves aren't? You can:

- Apply removable wallpaper or sticky-back vinyl paper to the shelves and insides of the drawers.
- Apply lino remnants or shelf liners (that can bought from the store).
- Use washi tape to decorate the fronts of the shelves.

APPLY STICKY-BACK VINYL (CONTACT PAPER) OR REMOVABLE WALLPAPER

This can be applied to the fronts of doors (if you decide to keep them on). There are actually companies out there that design custom vinyl panels to fit specific types of kitchen cupboard doors. You can go for patterned or plain vinyl to cover your doors (or both). This method works best on smooth doors that don't have any grooves.

You can also apply paper to the backs and/or insides of cupboards to spruce them up and make them a bit more 'you'. There's nothing quite like a good colour pop!

There's nothing quite like a good colour pop!

THE COUNTER TOPS

To most people, countertops are not exciting. But they are often the first thing you see when you walk into a kitchen, especially if they are chipped, peeling or damaged. In some homes, you'll also find countertops around the bathroom sink. Here's my guide for how to update them.

OPTION 1: REPLACE THE COUNTERS

Laugh. No. Just no.

OPTION 2: COVER WITH STICKY-BACK VINYL PAPER

OK, so I know sticky-back vinyl paper isn't the answer to a renter's every problem…
Ha, who am I kidding?

It is the solution. Sticky-back vinyl paper is the solution to ALL the problems, including this age-old 'mycounter tops are old, scratched and don't match my décor, and I need to find an affordable way to update them without upsetting
my landlord' dilemma.

So, sticky-back vinyl paper it is, then.

WHAT TYPES WORK?

When choosing the right sticky-back vinyl paper for your countertops, limit your choices to the more heavy-duty, high-quality type that you know will withstand whatever you decide to throw at it. Marble, wood grains and granite papers look the most authentic when applied, so I would suggest using those.

Sticky-back vinyl paper will work on most common types of countertop material such as laminate or marble, but I would be a little cautious about applying them directly to natural wooden counter tops. These surfaces require quite a high level of maintenance and care, so it's best to leave them exposed. If the wooden countertops in your kitchen are damaged in any way, a light sanding and reoiling will make them look like new again.

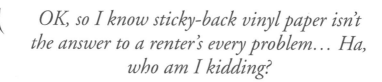

OK, so I know sticky-back vinyl paper isn't the answer to a renter's every problem… Ha, who am I kidding?

APPLYING CONTACT PAPER TO COUNTERTOPS

This is a very similar method to applying removable wallpaper (see page 32).

1. Clean the countertop surfaces with household cleaner and let them dry.
2. Once you have measured and cut your contact paper, line up the edge of the paper with the back of the counter (you can always overlap pieces if your paper isn't wide enough).
3. Slowly peel away the backing with one hand and use an old credit card to smooth out the bubbles with the other.
4. Trim off any excess paper and fold each corner in on itself.
5. Apply caulking (sealant) to the vinyl paper around the sink, or any other areas that may come into contact with water. And you're done!

THINGS TO KNOW

- Modern-day vinyl paper is usually quite durable and, in most cases, doesn't need an additional coat of varnish to protect it (if you were to use varnish, it would need to be a food-safe type). However, avoid chopping or placing anything hot directly on its surface.

- To remove – apply heat and peel away. If you've applied caulking to the edges, you will need to cut that away before removing the paper.

OTHER WAYS TO UPDATE COUNTERTOPS

- Paint. Always make sure you get your landlord's permission before trying something like this, as it's not reversible. I would suggest using a countertop-specific painting kit, which can be bought from most major online stores. Prices will vary, depending on the brand, but, overall, this product may seem expensive (although not as expensive as buying new counters – and I would also recommend you point that out to your landlord, should you ever need to pop the painting question). The kit will contain everything you need to paint your countertops. Some kits even have decorative chips inside that mimic the effects of popular finishes for an even more realistic, textured look.

- Add large chopping boards (for the kitchen). This is not really an update, but more of a disguise. You can cover up any damaged areas on your countertops with beautiful wooden boards or even trays.

APPLIANCES

When I talk about appliances, I mean the washing machine, the tumble dryer, the refrigerator…

Technically, these aren't what you'd call permanent features, but if they have been provided by your landlord, they are usually there to stay for the long haul.

No matter how grubby or dated they look, unless they actually don't work, these appliances aren't going anywhere. Which can make them a real eyesore.

In some homes, the washing machine and dryer will have their own separate quarters. Fancy, I know. However, in most instances, the washing machine is housed in the kitchen under the counter. When placed here, they are, of course, a lot harder to disguise.

But we shall try anyway.

Here are some fun ways to do that with – you guessed it – removable products.

Unless they actually don't work, these appliances aren't going anywhere. Which can make them a real eyesore.

MAKE STRIPES

For a striking but easy look, create vertical or horizontal stripes across your refrigerator with washi tape or masking tape. Use contrasting colours – a bold monochrome look works really well.

COVER IT UP

Want to go all out? Try covering your appliance face completely with a patterned removable wallpaper or sticky-back vinyl adhesive. See page 32 for guidance on how to apply it.

CREATE A CHALKBOARD

Add chalkboard paper to the face or sides of the refrigerator and get scribbling. Create your own temporary artworks, or just stay organized with a to-do list.

USE REFRIGERATOR MAGNETS

Brightly coloured children's letters are not the only magnets out there. Spruce up the front of your refrigerator with stylish magnets, including souvenirs from your trips abroad or prints from art galleries and museums. There are even companies that print personal photos directly into magnet form.

MAGNETIC STEEL

You could also try applying sheets of removable magnetic steel to the fronts of appliances (particularly refrigerators and dishwashers). These provide an instant update, and can be removed easily.

HIDE THE APPLIANCE

If in doubt, why not try simply hiding your appliance behind some curtains? This is a really clever way of concealing old appliances under the countertops. I mentioned them previously and on the next few pages I'm going to show you how to make your own.

PROJECT #16

NO-SEW CURTAIN CABINET SKIRT

What to do if your appliances are really beyond improvement? Simple – just cover them up. Creating a cabinet skirt to sit under your counter is the perfect way to hide unsightly appliances such as dishwashers or washing machines.

SUPPLIES

- Measuring tape
- Fabric of your choice
- Scissors
- Iron
- Sewing pins (optional)
- Iron-on hemming tape, 12mm (½in) wide
- Tension rod (make sure it is less than 5cm (2in) in circumference

A few things to note:

- A quick word about tension rods. Tension rods are a convenient way to hang lightweight curtains (or other items) between two points. They work by twist-to-expand/shorten mechanism, making them fairly easy to install. You don't need to drill holes or purchase any additional hardware to hang them. Remember to purchase a rod that is slightly wider than the space you want it for (tension rods lose their strength the more they are expanded), and then shorten to fit.
- For this project, you could use a pair of old bedsheets or curtains with hems already in place. Just cut to size and create a channel at the top for the tension rod.
- Alternatively, curtain hooks with clips can be used, if you don't want to create a rod channel.

1

Measure the width and length of the space where you intend to hang the curtain. Double the width measurement, or triple it if you want a fuller, more gathered curtain. Add 15cm (6in) to the length, to allow for the fabric being folded over at the top channel for the tension rod and the hem.

2

Lay your chosen fabric out on a flat surface to make it easier to keep lines straight, and measure and mark it to the right dimensions for your curtains. Cut it to size with your scissors.

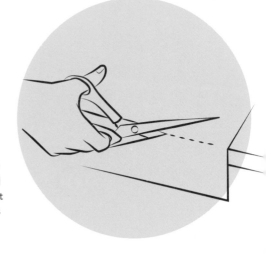

3

Hem the vertical sides of the fabric piece or pieces to hide the raw edges. To do this, fold 2cm (¾in) of fabric over at the edges so that the back or 'wrong' sides are together. Press with an iron to create a crease. Fold over again and use the iron to press the crease in place. Add pins to secure if your fabric doesn't hold a crisp line.

4

Now you need to hem the two vertical sides of your fabric. Place the fabric right side facing down on the ironing board. Cut the hemming tape to the same length as the folded edges. Working on one section at a time, slip the tape between the folded fabric so that it is covered and won't stick to your iron. Iron it in place, according to the manufacturer's instructions. Continue in this way until one side of the fabric is complete. Repeat on the other side.

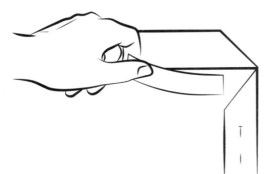

5

Begin the rod channel. Measure the circumference of your rod, then add 2.5cm (1in) to this measurement. This will be the width of your channel – mine was 7.5cm (3in). Fold the top 2cm (¾in) of the fabric to the wrong side and iron to crease. Stick this hem down with tape, as described in step 4, opposite.

6

Measure and mark a line below the top hemmed edge, according to your channel width measurement. I marked a line 7.5cm (3in) down. Fold the fabric over along the line so that the wrong sides are together, and iron a crease. Cut a length of hemming tape to the same width as your fabric. Position the tape under the hemmed edge of the rod channel and iron it in place.

7

Push the rod through the channel to check it fits properly. If you have any problems, you may be able to unstick the hemming tape by applying heat again, depending on the brand.

8

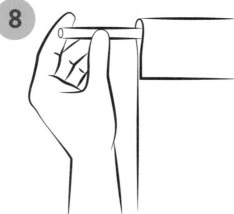

Hang the curtain up and then pin the bottom edge to the correct length. Take the curtain down carefully, and use your iron to crease the fabric at the hem line. Remove the pins. If you have a lot of folded-over fabric, trim it down so that only about 5cm (2in) remains, to reduce bulk. Hem the bottom edge in the same way as you hemmed the sides (see steps 3 and 4, opposite).

THE OTHER NOT-SO-PRETTY FIXTURES

I do appreciate the purpose of radiators, I really do. During the colder months, when all I do is hibernate (on the sofa) and eat my own body weight in comfort food, I am thankful for the heat they provide. I am grateful for a warm and cosy house. However, that doesn't change the fact that they can sometimes be quite ugly to look at.

Radiators always seem to be positioned in the most noticeable places (under the window, perhaps), which makes them much harder to conceal. Of course, there are some fancy-looking radiators out there that will blend oh-so effortlessly into a well-designed room. The good news: you probably could afford to buy said fancy radiator if you were to make a deal with yourself that 'no-spend January' was going to be the theme for every month for the next two years. The bad news: I doubt your landlord would be too impressed. Especially if you decided to get nifty with costs and install it yourself. Bodge job alert!

The phrase 'between a rock and a hard place' might be apt here. Hence why I'm about to give you some renter-friendly alternatives:

RADIATOR COVERS

Personally, I'm not a huge fan of radiator covers. I feel they take up far too much space, block heat (the very heat I already mentioned I was thankful for) and just scream, 'Look at me! I'm a radiator cover!' Which kind of defeats the purpose, right?

But, in the interests of trying to sound less biased, I will admit that radiator covers can work for you if you want them to. There are lots of designs that are sold through most major homeware stores that can be customized to your style.

NARROW ENTRANCE TABLES

You might have seen those pictures on Pinterest, where a clever homeowner has used very long hairpin legs (other kinds of legs are available) and attached them to a beautiful piece of wood. This 'table' is then placed over a radiator and no one is the wiser. I like it.

RADIATOR SHELVES/LEDGES

Place a shelf at a height just above your radiator. This can be attached directly to the wall or it can fit on brackets that slot behind the radiator. As well as being a great way to detract attention from the eyesore that is a radiator, shelves installed this way are said to make rooms warmer as they deflect the rising heat. I call that killing two birds with one stone.

PAINT

This is an option I have tried many times and would highly recommend. It's simple to do and, best of all, it's cost-effective. Most of the properties I've rented have had radiators that were yellowing from a build-up of dirt and grease over the years. A thorough clean and a coat of fresh white paint will change that in an instant. Rule of thumb, if you are looking to disguise your radiator, then it's a good idea to paint it the same colour as the wall (which is usually white or ghastly magnolia). Ideally, radiators should be removed from the wall before painting, but honestly, who's got time for that? See below for how to go about it.

HOW TO PAINT A RADIATOR

1. Always make sure you turn the heating off before you paint a radiator – it needs to be completely cold.
2. Lay out some dustsheets or old bedsheets around the radiator to protect the floor, and then slide some old cardboard behind it to avoid getting any paint on the walls.
3. Clean the radiator with a household cleaner to get rid of any dirt or debris.
4. Lightly sand the radiator to remove any lumps of paint or rust.
5. Prime the radiator with radiator-specific or metal primer (unless you are painting a radiator that has already had a few coats of paint applied, in which case a primer might not be needed).
6. Apply the top coat with a brush, ideally using a radiator-specific paint. If that's not available, use any paint designed for metal.

THE BATHROOM

So, your bath panel is chipped, the shower head is covered in limescale and the air vent is an unsightly horror on the wall. Is there any point even trying to make your rented bathroom look good? Luckily, there are some handy tricks that will make a huge improvement. And remember to refer to pages 38–41 for ways to update the wall tiles.

CHANGE THE BATH PANEL

Some rental properties will have a straight-edged bath installed in the bathroom. This bath will have a side panel to disguise unsightly plumbing and pipework. If this panel is damaged in any way (or you simply want something a little more stylish), this panel can usually be removed and replaced without the need of a professional. Online video tutorials might be the best way to go about learning how to do this. The process usually involves trimming the panel to size and slipping it back in place.

Nowadays, bath panels come in a variety of colours and styles, so think of this as an on-budget way to transform a boring bathroom. Personally, I love the tongue-and-groove type of panels – they add a little classic glamour.

There is, however, one downside to this solution – not every home you rent will have a straight-edged bath. Shower baths have curved side panels that are a little trickier to fit and, of course, freestanding baths don't have side panels at all.

COVER THE BATH PANEL WITH REMOVABLE PAPER OR STICKY-BACK VINYL

As long as you are using a removable wallpaper that is bathroom specific or, at the very least, glossy and wipeable, there is no reason why your bath panel cannot be given a refresh in this way.

ADD GLITZ

A lady shared a glitter bath-panel tutorial on my blog once. She mixed glitter and PVA glue together, applied it to her panel and sealed everything with clear car lacquer. Apparently, it's holding up well! I just thought I'd throw this alternate option out there, in case you're the kind of person who likes glitz and glamour in your life.

BUY YOURSELF A STEP

One last thing on baths: if your bathtub has quite high sides, and climbing in can sometimes become a safety hazard, buy yourself a cute little step.

THE SHOWER HEAD

Replacing a shower head is a great way to improve the overall look of a bathroom – especially if the current shower head is grotty, covered in limescale and has a weak water flow. However, a word of caution: permission needs to be sought from your landlord beforehand, as there may be a plumbing clause in your contract that forbids this. Also, if you aren't skilled at DIY, a qualified plumber will need to install this for you.

THE AIR VENTS

If your air vents are in use, you shouldn't be covering or blocking them in any way. However, new, prettier-looking covers can improve their overall appearance.

If the air vent is not in use or broken, consider covering it over with a picture frame or large canvas artwork. If the vents are low down on the wall, near the floor, you can position your furniture in a way that helps to conceal them.

THE THERMOSTAT (OR OTHER ELECTRONIC GIZMOS)

This is usually quite an unattractive-looking device, placed in the most obvious of locations and always at eye level. You could invest in a more streamlined-looking model, but at a cost. So disguising it (and I realize that I've most likely killed this word for you by using it 12,133 times in this chapter already) might be your best bet. Here are a few ideas:

- Cover it with a removable object such as a box, basket or stylish hat.

- Camouflage it within an awesome gallery wall.

- Install a shelf or ledge below it and hide it behind picture fames or other decorations.

- Attach some small hinges to a canvas frame and place it over the thermostat. This swing mechanism will allow you to easily access your thermostat when needed.

It's important to keep in mind, though, that if you are choosing to cover your thermostat, you might not always get an accurate reading of the room temperature reading due to a lack of air circulation.

RESOURCES

WOOD

Buy plywood from stores such as Jewson and B&Q. You can also source secondhand wood from The Freecycle Network, eBay or Gumtree.

www.jewson.co.uk
www.diy.com
www.freecycle.org
www.ebay.com
www.gumtree.com

BUILDING SUPPLIES

In the UK, my go-to places for buying building supplies are Screwfix and B&Q. In the US, you can buy from Lowe's or The Home Depot.

www.screwfix.com
www.diy.com
www.lowes.com
www.homedepot.com

PAINT

For painting furniture, I would recommend using Rust-Oleum or Valspar Emulsion. For walls, I would use Valspar or Dulux.

www.rustoleum.com
www.valsparpaint.co.uk
www.dulux.co.uk

REMOVABLE WALLPAPER

You can buy removable paper from ColoRay, Spoonflower, Astek Home and Walls Need Love.

www.coloraydecor.com
www.Spoonflower.com
www.astekhome.com
www.wallsneedlove.com

FABRIC

Spoonflower have a wide rage of fabric prints (the rug on page 67 is made from a fabric from their watercolour selection). You can also design your own fabrics and get them printed on to different materials. They ship worldwide.

www.Spoonflower.com

ART

You can download and print custom art for gallery walls from Etsy.Desenio sell a selection of different prints, at reasonable prices, and Print Club London sell limited edition screenprints

www.etsy.com
www.desenio.co.uk
www.printclublondon.com

INTERIORS AND HOMEWARE

Ikea is great for affordable, flat-pack furniture, as well as wooden crates, frames, bedding, rugs or artificial plants. Try West Elm for modern, stylish furniture pieces that will prove a great investment. Maison du Monde sell budget-friendly, quirky items and rugs. Go to Iconic Lights for wall lights and floor lamps, and H&M Home for bedding, baskets and home accessories. You can also buy picture frames from eBay and rugs from Homesense.

www.ikea.com
www.westelm.com
www.maisondumonde.com
www.iconiclights.com
www.hm.com
www.ebay.com
www.homesense.com

INSPIRATION

Find inspiration in magazines such as *Elle Decoration*, *Elle Décor* and *Living Etc*. Instagram is also always a good place to find inspiration.

Elsie and Emma at A Brilliant Mess have great home décor and craft ideas. Mandy at Vintage Revivals is the queen of awesome feature walls, and Francesca at Fall For DIY has lots of easy, modern DIY ideas (and we share a studio space!).

www.elledecor.com
www.livingetc.com
www.abeautifulmess.com
www.vintagerevivals.com
www.fallfordiy.com

INDEX

ACKNOWLEDGEMENTS

Thank you to Vincent, my husband, my soulmate, my best friend. Without you, this book may never have been possible. Your patience and continued support throughout the good, the bad and the really bad days was really what got me through this whole process. You came home to sinks full of dishes, last-minute takeaway meals and piles of unwashed laundry and didn't bat an eyelid. You got stuck in, without question and always put my worries and fears to rest. You've taught me everything I know about DIY. I love you. You and our beautiful boy are my world.

To Ella, my super amazing Editor who had all the patience of a holy person. Thank you. I know I wasn't the easiest to work with. My snail pace method of working would have put many off, but not you. And we've done it. I can't believe it!

Special thanks to my Dad, who really helped shape and edit some of the initial ideas for this book. And to Mum, I'm pretty sure my love for interior design came from you. Coming home from school to well-placed furniture and beautiful, styled spaces has been the inspiration for many of my own designs. You were the very first person to teach me how to create a home.

To lifelong friends like Laina and Rabab – I can always count on you both to help and support, even if we are miles apart. To Rida, who I met online and who has become such a good friend, you kept me on track. Those nights out we took for a little self love were a godsend – would this book have been written without them?

To my sister Saara, my son really does have the best aunty. My last-minute requests for babysitting while I wrote this book helped more than you will ever know. Thank you!

To Fran, from Fall For DIY and also my studio partner. You might have noticed I 'borrowed' a few of your gorgeous makes and props for some of the imagery in this book. I don't think this book would been half as special without them. To Kasia, our photographer on the day, thank you for all the beautiful shots of my DIY projects. I can't think of anyone better to have worked with on this.

And most of all, thank you to YOU! – readers, Instagram followers, facebook group members, loyal blog subscribers, colleagues and friends! You are one of the reasons this book is even possible and in buying this book, you have helped fulfil a life long dream for me. And to my fellow renters, I hear you, I see you. You aren't alone on this journey.

ABOUT THE AUTHOR

Medina Grillo is the voice behind the blog Grillo Designs, where she shares creative and affordable ways to decorate your home with a DIY approach. The blog has gained a large readership over the years and has won some prestigious awards, including the 2017 Best DIY and Home Improvement Blog by Amara, and *domino* magazine's Pinner's Choice Award 2017. Her DIY tutorials have been featured in a variety of both online and print publications, such as *Real Homes, Make It Yours, Apartment Therapy* and the *Telegraph*. Her goal is to inspire creativity and her tagline is: 'Just your average renter, making a house a home!'

For Information on Medina:
Blog: www.grillodesigns.com
Instagram: www.instagram.com/grillodesigns
Youtube: www.youtube.com/grillodesigns

Share and follow #HowIRent and #HomeSweetRentedHome to connect with other renters online, and to celebrate all the amazing ways to transform a rented space.

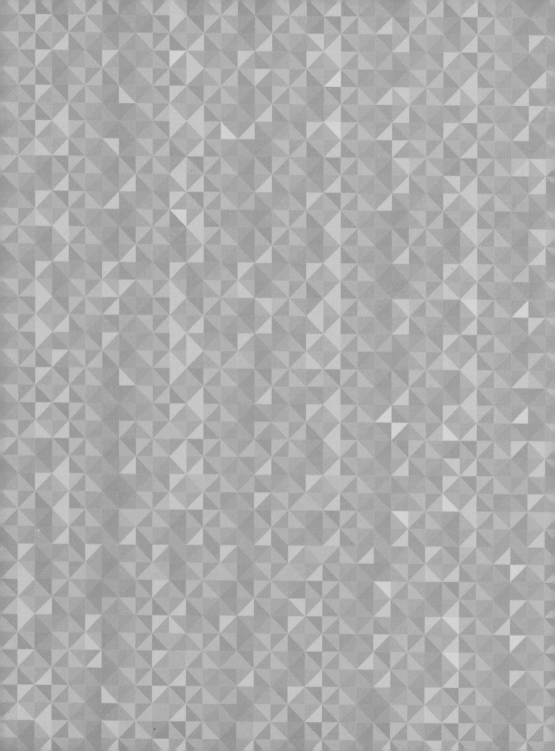